POWER, INTEREST
AND
PSYCHOLOGY

Reviews of *Power, Interest and Psychology*

When I first read David Smail it was because a reviewer had said that Smail was 'psychology's Voltaire'. I was intrigued. Could Smail's work match the fearless satire of the 17th-century genius? The answer ... was yes ... The book is irreverent and destructive (or perhaps I should say 'deconstructive'), but it is powerfully and originally constructive too.

Challenging, disturbing, revelatory and genuinely original, Smail's work has had too little influence to date on the world of academic and professional psychology. Perhaps this is because it is ... 50 years ahead of its time and doesn't satisfy our contemporary demand for 'serious' (that is, tunnel-visioned ... introverted) psychology. There's a surging current of analysis here that should be read by all students of psychology. And it is beautifully written. It represents a rare thing amongst the dross that is churned out.

Professor Gary Thomas, University of Birmingham
The Psychologist, October 2005

The central tenet of Smail's argument is that society and the interests of materialism and marketing are the determining factors inhibiting the health and happiness of the individual. Autonomy, will-power and self-change are concepts the powerless majority believe they possess, when in fact it is society that has ultimate power over our well-being.

A powerful case is made for counselling and psychotherapy training to encompass more research experience as well as including a substantial element of training in social psychotherapy. His complex and careful assessment of social machinations is ... more convincing than his view that therapy offers 'absolutely no help' in allowing individuals to make personal change. Nonetheless his suggestion that therapists need a fuller understanding of the social system in which they and their clients are tied up is one which as a social psychotherapist I fully endorse. The surprise is that it has been overlooked for so long in so many training courses.

Angela Cooper, psychotherapist
CPJ, October 2005

Reviews of *Power, Interest and Psychology*

David Smail must feel like for years he's been beating his fists against the interior walls of a sound-proofed chamber; that chamber of course being professional psychology and therapy … he's not only kicked at the partitions—hoping to impact on the smug goings-on in the rooms next door—but also called the world outside, exasperated by society's injustices … intent on … exposing the dusty ornaments for the fakes they are.

… But despite the crimes it has committed, Smail wants not to abandon psychology but to rescue it:

'The psychologist's job at this—and, I believe, at any other—time is not to *diagnose* the 'inner person' but to *explicate* his or her relationship with the outside world. This is to switch 'professional' attention from discipline and conformity to a libertarian concern with understanding subjective distress as a function of the personal (and ultimately, of course, wider) environment' (p. 68, original emphasis).

Andy Rogers
Ipnosis, review article, Autumn 2006

POWER, INTEREST AND PSYCHOLOGY

Elements of a social materialist understanding of distress

DAVID SMAIL

PCCS Books
Ross-on-Wye

First published in 2005
Reprinted 2007
Reprinted 2009

PCCS BOOKS
2 Cropper Row
Alton Road
ROSS-ON-WYE
HR9 5LA
UK
Tel +44 (0)1989 763 900
contact@pccs-books.co.uk
www.pccs-books.co.uk

Power, Interest and Psychology:
Elements of a social materialist understanding of distress

British Library Cataloguing in Publication Data.
A catalogue record for this book is available from the British
Library.

ISBN 978 1 898059 71 4

Cover designed in the UK by The Old Dog's Missus
Printed in the UK by ImprintDigital.net

Contents

To the memory of Roger Poole

Introduction

When I was very young, and optimism about 'science' was at its height, I used to worry that by the time I grew up there would be nothing left in the world to discover and that I would be redundant as a thinking being. Well, I needn't have worried: now that I am considerably older, it seems to me that the world I inhabit has never been so sunk in superstition and ignorance.

The ironies are unending. The idealism that led me to study psychology was partly founded on a feeling that here, at least, there were still mysteries to be unravelled. In fact, as it turns out, psychology—all unknowing—has done more to mystify the human condition than just about any other even remotely intellectual enterprise.

As I grew up in the 1950s—as callow a youth as any of that era—the post-war world was pretty grey and Spartan, but there was nevertheless (or so it seems to me now) a general belief in the possibility of improving the lot of common humanity—if not on a global scale, at least on the home front. A Labour government had come to power that, whatever its shortcomings, addressed inequality and injustice in a way that seems extraordinarily radical as against the dishonest manipulations of today's 'New Labour'. There were real jobs for people to do and an optimistic belief in the benefits of health and education for all. Much to the discomfort of some of the more affluent sections of the population (to which most of the people I knew aspired even though they didn't belong), it seemed that the snobbery and privilege so characteristic of pre-war British society were on their way out for good. Even if vestiges of it lingered here and there, it seemed that Bertie Wooster's world was dead.

But it wasn't. Though wise enough not to draw too much attention to itself, it continued more or less unabated among significant minorities of the population, and nostalgic memories of its glories festered resentfully in the psyches of those who were only too soon to mount the Thatcherist counter-revolution. And now we've got it all back with—literally—a vengeance.

The 'Twenty-First Century' which politicians and tabloids love to invoke as emblematic of progress, is culturally and economically a rewind to the between-the-wars society so many of us hoped we'd seen the back of: a world in which a greedy and self-satisfied middle class re-establishes and ostentatiously celebrates the advantages of its parasitism on those who really produce the goods.

Not that nothing has changed—the mechanics of exploitation and privilege are far less crude than they used to be, and far less apparent to even the interested onlooker. The principal locations of exploitation have been moved, through the apparatus of 'globalisation', to where most of us can't see them and don't really care about them even if we can. The mass of the population, no longer so obviously belittled and patronised by its 'betters', is pacified by the de-regulation of pleasure and stupefied by the relentless 'dumbing down' of information. The depth of perspective of even the educated class has been reduced to the span of no more than a few years, making it less and less easy to understand how and why societal change comes about.

And in all this 'psychology'—a central tool of ideological power—plays its crucial part. If people are to be diverted from criticising the material circumstances that condition their lives, they must believe those circumstances to be irrelevant, and psychology has over the past century invented and sustained a magical theology in which it seems that people may choose them*selves* and shape their future by eradicating their past. Tragedy may be averted by no more, essentially, than wishing that things might be otherwise, and reality is reduced to a set of stories that may be manipulated to result in happy endings.

The only thing that people are called upon to *do* to realise their dreams is to *consume*, and psychology has been fundamental to the creation of the perfect consumer. The latter is an individual detached from every kind of social and environmental context other than that of greedy competition for goods and services with other individuals, existing otherwise in a fantasy world where there is *in theory* no limit to the achievement of gratification.

It is precisely in establishing the theory that psychology has been so influential. One of the central problems that faces the limitless 'growth' on which capitalism depends is the restrictions placed by material circumstances on what we can achieve—restrictions, that is, that arise out of our physical environment, our physical bodies and the existence of other people. These have to be dematerialised, changed from potential barriers into sites and objects of desire, where limitless aims may be attained through acts of consumption which are, crucially, mediated by essentially *mental* processes such as wishing and deciding—and dreaming. The modern consumer is in this way a pleasure-seeking idealist, dislocated from a real world, a real body and a real society. We must believe, among other things, that the earth's resources are infinite, that mind will triumph over matter and that there's no limit to what you can achieve if you really try. Psychology helps a lot in this enterprise.

One should be careful, however, about using the word 'psychology' too loosely, as it covers a wide range of academic and professional activities, many of which have very little in common with each other. The kind of psychology I am concerned with in this book is essentially the 'clinical' variety, which takes for its subject matter the broad field of 'mental health' and evolved from a mixture of behavioural learning theory, 'dynamic' (in particular psychoanalytic) psychologies and the so called 'humanistic' psychologies of the mid-twentieth century. It is in many respects closely similar to—and indeed for the purposes of my argument includes—other approaches to 'psychotherapy' and 'counselling' and is as concerned as they to establish *professional* credentials. 'Psychology' of this kind is no longer an intellectual discipline, a branch of philosophy or science, but seeks recognition as a protected, technical profession with established procedures for the treatment of psychological disorders. It is taught not to *students*, but to *trainees*, and it will soon be illegal for anyone to call him or herself a 'psychologist' unless officially registered as such.

As I have already suggested, the claim to objectively established validity implied in this professional stance is entirely without foundation in anything other than a carefully constructed mythology which has much in common with many other branches of 'knowledge' in the twenty-first-century world, not least the 'postmodernist' flights of many influential philosophical and cultural commentators, as well as theorists in some other branches of non-clinical psychology. I will say no more at this stage about why this should be so—I hope the reasons will become apparent as the argument progresses.

The dilemma facing me at this juncture is to find a name for what *I* am doing!

It's hard to see how I can avoid 'psychology' at least as *part* of my enterprise, as there is no doubt that that has been the discipline that has had most influence over the field to be considered. But it does have terribly misleading connotations and built-in assumptions—for example that we are concerned primarily with what goes on inside people's heads or 'psyches' (with what I shall call the world of 'ideality'). In fact we are concerned at least as much with people's worlds. Not to mention their bodies.

The terms 'therapeutic' psychology and 'psychotherapy' are also profoundly unsatisfactory, for the kind of human distress with which we are concerned has nothing to do with illness or treatment. The analogy with 'therapy' and 'treatment' has already misled us for over a century.

'Clinical' psychology is problematic because of its similarly unfortunate association with medicine, and also because clinical psychology has, as indicated, become a *technical* profession, like chiropody or dietetics, that focuses on the pragmatics of relief rather than on any more abstract intellectual or scientific enterprise. Clinical psychology has given up any serious attempt to *explain*.

'Counselling' looks like quite a good term on the face of it, but has become ineradicably associated with the professional provision of a quite circumscribed form of psychological help, based in particular on understandings of Carl Rogers's approach to 'client-centred therapy'. Although there are brave attempts to rescue counselling from this conceptual dead-end (for example Alex Howard's work),[1] they are in my view unlikely to be successful: counsellors are too set on becoming established professionals.

In many ways sociology and anthropology might seem to offer a more appropriate home, but their focus is too broad: despite an hostility towards individual*ism*, I am still focally concerned with individual experience.

I think perhaps—under protest, so to speak—I'm stuck with 'psychology', but tacitly hedged round with all the qualifications I've mentioned.

Ultimately, our[2] concern is with human subjectivity, with the experience of being a person, and in particular with the types of suffering and pain that being a person can engender. Perhaps I should say *avoidable* pain and suffering, for otherwise our project becomes at once too grandiose and too simplistic: much suffering and pain is inevitable in a human lifetime, and may be understood and endured in many ways, many of them nothing to do with any branch of psychology.

The avoidable pain and suffering that forms the focus of our attention is not a 'mental' thing, but arises from our nature as embodied beings. But neither would it solve our problem to search for the origin and end of our suffering— as so much of psychiatry has done—simply in our biogenetic make up.[3] For we are bodies in a world: of course (and very importantly) in a physical world, but also a socially structured, material space-time in which what we do to each other has enormous importance.

The strength and integrity of the subject is determined not (as therapeutic psychology would have us believe) by efforts of individual will, but by the adequacy or otherwise of the environment (including, crucially, the public societal structures) in which it is located.

Where public structures are stable, supportive and nurturing, the spirit may blossom and flourish; where they disintegrate (where 'all that is solid melts into air')[4] the subject becomes shrivelled and reduced to its biological elements of survival. A culture adequate to the blooming of subjectivity constitutes a form of enchantment[5] born of our benign social collusion in buttressing ourselves against the harshness of our place in the universe to make it habitable in peace and civility. To destroy that enchantment is (rather like stripping the flesh from the steel skeleton of the Terminator) to reduce ourselves to our animal nature, revealing an asocial set of ruthlessly competitive individuals. The most pitiless of these rise to the top as a kind of aggregation of oppression (a 'band of brigands')[6] while the most fragile and sensitive sink to the bottom, struggling anxiously for survival, as (needfully!) paranoid as little birds that hardly dare to snatch a crumb for fear of failing to spot the stooping hawk or the crouching cat.

That is why social Darwinism comes to the fore at times when the brigands are in charge: the focus on human 'nature'[7] as the basis for communal living, the Thatcherite repudiation of 'society' and the glorification of selfishness and competition reflect accurately enough the state of a disenchanted world.

What kind of world we want is an *ethical* choice: the attempt to establish one or another as somehow *necessarily* more desirable or right is never likely to succeed—hence, perhaps, the inevitability of the political split between Left and Right. There is no indisputably objective or technical reason why we should consider or try to alleviate the individual's experience of pain. People can and often do ignore or deny their common humanity with others, or deny, at least implicitly, that their common humanity commits them to any sympathy or compassion for those less advantaged than themselves. Indeed, such an attitude towards one's fellows can be represented as tough, uncompromising, positively heroic: the supermen versus the wimps.[8] But just as this ruthless world may be chosen—as it is chosen by the current rulers of the globalised neo-liberal market—so may it also be rejected.

This book is founded on just such a rejection. I'm siding with the wimps. We are not bound to accept that the 'real world' is one in which the 'bottom line' defines and determines right and wrong. We do not have to acquiesce in the impoverished vocabulary and banal ideological apparatus of institutional Business culture. We do not, furthermore, have to be intimidated by the more sophisticated intellectual apologists for postmodernism and the free market to be found in various academic nests like the London School of Economics. Our undertaking, in contrast, rests on a compassionate solidarity with others, and the fact that this is fundamentally and irreducibly an *ethical* choice does not mean it is in any way irrational (like many others, I have argued elsewhere[9] that reason and ethics are not—and certainly do not have to be—separable from each other).

While what founds and fuels our enquiry is a moral position, the enquiry itself must be an essentially *scientific* one. By 'science' I do not mean the rigid, dogmatic, 'positivist' orthodoxy so rightly reviled by the postmodernists. I mean rather the kind of open, inquisitive, sceptical, empirical approach that keeps itself free of dogmatism by seeking to refer back constantly to an intellectual peer group of men and women who are both *informed* and of *good will* (Habermas).[10]

Power, Interest and Psychology

In struggling to elucidate the mysteries of the world and our relations to it, science has to acknowledge that its enquiries cannot be so objective as to be completely uninfluenced by our own interests, preoccupations and biological characteristics (Habermas,[11] Polanyi).[12] At the same time, however, it strives for *evidence* that is *as far as possible* free from conceptual and empirical mistakes and ideological distortions of one kind or another (e.g. religious or political—including 'politically correct'—biases). Science is about our passionate conviction that we are placed within a universe that is not simply the result of our own imaginings, and our longing and determination to understand it. Ultimately, science is about reality, truth and freedom.

Our part is to occupy a tiny corner of this enterprise: i.e., to attempt to grasp and elucidate some of the ways in which human beings are brought to suffer avoidable distress. Much of this book is the continuation of a search I have been engaged in now for several years for a language—a set of concepts— which may offer us a better way of thinking about this field than has so far been available; a language, that is to say, that makes sense of our suffering, that may enable us to place it within a real world and perhaps even to begin to get a grip on it.

Most of the themes considered in these pages, and indeed a good deal of the text, originated in the 'Internet publication' *Power, Responsibility and Freedom* that I developed on my website over the past five years or so.[13] I undertook that project in the hope that writing on the Internet would allow both a continuous interaction with readers and the possibility of maintaining a fluid, changing text that, freed from the constraints of paper and ink, could keep pace with changes of mind as well as changes in circumstances. In the event, however, the outcome of this experiment has been fairly disappointing.

Although I have no idea how many people actually read the web pages, I do know that very few people indeed actually responded to them in the way that I had hoped—a mere handful. I suspect that reading lengthy texts on the Internet is not something many people choose to do, and downloading and printing out, apart from being somewhat tedious and expensive, does not carry the same satisfaction as handling or owning a book. Published books, moreover, however unwarrantedly, carry with them a kind of authority that is lacking in Internet texts: the very freedom of expression that is such an attractive feature of the Web is also a drawback to those who need to feel—possibly quite unconsciously—that what they are reading has at least *some* kind of official endorsement.

It only became apparent after a couple of years or so that what had seemed another advantage of Web writing—its topicality—turns all too quickly into a disadvantage, or at least a burden on the writer. The instancy and fluidity of electronic text makes it possible to refer to other publications and events within minutes of their occurrence, and this can make for exhilarating writing—and reading. Many excellent news, current affairs and activist websites attest to this huge benefit of the Internet. But for an amateur Web-writer such as myself, material written in the heat of the moment becomes stale surprisingly quickly and unless one constantly updates the text one is left with a production far too obviously reliant on yesterday's news. Books, in contrast, are written in full awareness of the relative permanence of the printed page.

Although, then, much of the material in these pages can be traced to *Power Responsibility and Freedom*, it has been fundamentally reorganised and greatly augmented. I have removed many of the topical asides that may still be found on the website and introduced new material (especially but not only in Chapter 2) that, I hope, carries my argument further. My resorting to a more formal medium of publication does not mean, however, that I would not welcome reader response, and I can still be contacted via the website.

David Smail
Nottingham

Notes

1. Alex Howard, 1996. *Challenges to Counselling and Psychotherapy,* Macmillan.; and 2000. *Philosophy for Counselling and Psychotherapy,* Macmillan.

2. I have found it difficult to decide whether to write mainly in the first person singular or the first person plural. In many ways I prefer the latter, but in the end the apparent assumption that writer and reader form a harmonious 'we' starts to sound laboured and patronising. Always to speak of 'I', however, strays almost as far in the direction of egotism. I have therefore tried to strike some kind of balance between the two, and I hope that the reader will bear with me if I have not entirely succeeded.

3. For an excellent critique of biological psychiatry see, Terry Lynch, 2004. *Beyond Prozac.* PCCS Books.

4. This observation of Marx's is treated at length by Marshall Berman, 1983. *All That is Solid Melts into Air.* Verso.

5. The concept of enchantment is discussed by Max Weber in his *The Protestant Ethic and the Spirit of Capitalism.* Unwin Paperbacks, 1985 (original edn 1930).

6. Expression used to telling effect by Robert Tressell in *The Ragged Trousered Philanthropists.*

7. For example Steven Pincher, 2002. *The Blank Slate.* Penguin.

8. For an academic exposition of this kind of viewpoint see John Gray's *Straw Dogs: on Humans and other Animals.* 2002, Granta. At a less rarefied intellectual level, Margaret Mitchell's character Rhett Butler, in a scene towards the end of *Gone With The Wind*, puts the

case for the ruthless swashbucklers and carpetbaggers of the world with surprising eloquence: it is they (the brigands) who are the heroes of chaos and disintegration, the carriers-forward of the race, while the likes of the pale and disorientated Ashley Wilkes quietly go to the wall, lost from a world from which the 'enchantment has vanished' (1974 edn, Pan Books pp.754–7).

9. Smail, D. 1993. *The Origins of Unhappiness*. HarperCollins. This work forms half of the double volume *The Nature of Unhappiness*. Robinson, 2001.

10. Habermas, J. 1987. *The Philosophical Discourse of Modernity*. Polity Press.

11. Habermas, J. 1978. *Knowledge and Human Interests*. Heinemann.

12. Polanyi, M. 1958. *Personal Knowledge*. Routledge & Kegan Paul.

13. www.davidsmail.freeuk.com/

1

Looking Back

Therapeutic psychology has been going long enough now for it to have a discernible history. The story of its development since the last quarter of the nineteenth century is in fact a familiar one and I am not going to repeat it here.[1] There are, however, just a few features of this story that I would like to pick out for particular comment.

The most striking thing of all is how 'psychotherapy', in becoming one of the greatest cultural and commercial success stories of the Western world, remained over the past hundred years almost hermetically sealed off from the rest of reality. It was in fact as if the world had split in two: the West introvertedly preoccupied with the workings of the individual psyche, the East extravertedly concerning itself with the machinery of material relations within society.

But it was not as though the real world wasn't happening as we Westerners searched for the meaning of our actions in our secret wishes and unconscious motives. The twentieth century, after all, exploded into revolution and war on an unprecedented scale, but you would hardly know it from examining the theoretical speculations of Freud and Jung at the time—and so far as outer events did concern them, it was nearly always as an expression of inner 'psychic' conflicts of some kind (a stance still widely evident among some psychoanalytic writers).[2]

This indifference to the mundane operation of external materiality by no means meant that the great psychologists were above such things—it was just that they appeared not to attach much psychological significance to them. It is a particularly poignant irony that Freud's concept of repression is probably the best explanation one can find for his apparently failing to notice the importance to him (and indeed to us all) of the means of material survival.

This is nowhere clearer than in the correspondence[3] Freud maintained with his friend Wilhelm Fliess during the years in which the foundations of psychoanalysis were laid. The extraordinary thing is (if hardly unexpected from common sense) that while refining a theory which carried its subjects further and further from the real concerns of an outer world, when it came to his personal life Freud over and over again in his letters betrayed a consuming anxiety about that most mundane of preoccupations: money.[4]

In his letter to Fliess of 2 November 1896, for example, Freud expresses worry about 'the state of my practice this year on which my mood always remains dependent'. While as an explanation of psychological unease this would have had the full understanding of almost any nineteenth-century European novelist, it seems not to have occurred to Freud to countenance such a material basis for the troubles of his patients.

However, his personal circumstances have improved somewhat by 6 December, 'after having for once enjoyed the full measure of work and earnings *that I need for my well-being* (ten hours and a hundred florins) …'.[5] And a couple of months later (8 February, 1897) things are even more promising:

> I now have ten patients in treatment, including one from Budapest; another one from Breslau is due to arrive. It is probably one hour too much, though otherwise I feel best precisely when I am working a lot. Last week, for example, I earned 700 florins—you don't get that for nothing. Getting rich must be very difficult.

In one of the most interesting letters in the collection (21 September, 1897)—that which announces to Fliess the beginnings of a shift in Freud's theory of neurosis, from the view that his patients were sexually molested as children to the idea that they imagined it all—there is a continuous theme of financial insecurity running alongside his reasons for abandoning some of his previously key contentions (e.g. that fathers could so often be involved in 'widespread perversions'). The letter opens with Freud's observation that he is '… impoverished, at present without work', and acknowledges later on that: 'The expectation of eternal fame was so beautiful, as was that of certain wealth, complete independence, travels, and lifting the children above the *severe worries that robbed me of my youth*.' Towards the end he regrets—prematurely as it turned out—that 'It is a pity that one cannot make a living … on dream interpretation!'

Jeffrey Masson, in his excellent account of this period of Freud's life,[6] suggests that Freud's retraction of the seduction theory and substitution of it with the idea that sexual events in the patient's past were fantasy, represented a failure of moral courage. But maybe one can see other, more tangible, more material factors at work here. Could it be that Freud's gradual shifting of the burden of blame for his patients' 'neuroses' from the fathers and uncles of his 'hysterical' female patients to, eventually, themselves (via, incidentally, the lower orders in their household—the servant girls), might have been something to do with who was paying his bills?

A letter of 21 September 1899—as fine a piece of self-analysis as one could wish for—would appear to give weight to the view that money was for Freud as strong a motivator as it is for most of the rest of us:

> A patient with whom I have been negotiating, a 'goldfish', has just announced herself—I do not know whether to decline or accept. *My mood also depends very strongly on my earnings. Money is laughing gas for me*. I know from my youth that once the wild horses of the pampas have been lassoed, they retain a certain anxiousness for life. Thus *I have come to know the helplessness of poverty and continually fear it*. You will see that my style will improve and my ideas will be more correct if this city provides me with an ample livelihood.

It would surely be very hard in these circumstances for Freud to pursue a theory that threatened to cut off the very source of his income.

It is perhaps a particularly twentieth-century form of prudery that money as a *personal* motivation is not something alluded to in polite society, and to 'accuse' Freud of being influenced by material concerns can still easily be taken as at least tasteless and at most outrageous. But is it not precisely outrage, indignation and accusations of unworthiness—the idea, in short, that some things are just too tasteless to suggest—which generates and masks the operations of repression?

What seems to me particularly significant is that a psychologist focally concerned with our most basic fears and motivations—one, moreover, famously given to self-analysis—should not find a fundamental place in his theoretical structure for factors '*on which my mood always remains dependent*', which he feels '*I need for my well-being*', and which created '*the severe worries that robbed me of my youth*'.

This may be revealing, but it need not be surprising. For what it reveals is not a shameful flaw in Freud's character, but the extent to which we all manage to avoid reference to the way our actions are governed by our interest—the way, that is, we need always and everywhere to struggle with and adjust to the material demands of our existence. And 'avoiding reference to' is precisely what is meant by repression, as Freud himself made very clear.[7]

In my view, the nineteenth-century theoretician who best understood the relation of people to their world, and what this meant (among other things) for their conscious as well as unconscious understanding of themselves, was Karl Marx. While 'dialectical materialism' helped fuel the struggles against oppression of the peoples of Eastern (and some of Western) Europe, the intellectual preoccupations and philosophical tastes of the intelligentsia to which the theories of Freud and Jung appealed were far more equivocal. One could not say that the founders of therapeutic psychology had no interest in material science, but that interest was always fused with a penchant for magical authority that attempted—and in a way largely succeeded in—lifting theory beyond the reach of empirical criticism. In this Freudians and Jungians typified a cultural strain already evident in the West for some time, and which flowered most colourfully at about the turn of the twentieth century in a strange mixture of scientific curiosity, fascination with the occult, aestheticism, religiosity and obsessive sexual interest and experimentation. This, of course, is what we tend to mean when we speak of *'fin de siècle'*.[8]

It is not hard to identify the currents in nineteenth-century literary and artistic, philosophical and scientific culture that resonated with the thought of Freud and his followers, and it is also of interest to note those that didn't. Both Freud and Jung, I would suggest, swim in the same stream as, for example, Nietzsche, Blavatsky and Yeats, the Pre-Raphaelites, Wagner, Bergson. In other words, theirs is a kind of amalgam of Romantic, occult, mystical and 'scientific' ideas, where, however, science is attractive more for the mysterious authority it may bestow than for its empirical transparency (witness, for example, Freud's enthusiasm for Charcot's hypnotism).

On the other hand, what one might call the materialist line of nineteenth-century culture—including (as more or less random examples) Dickens, Tolstoy and indeed most of the great English, Russian and French novelists, Proudhon, Marx, and slightly later writers like Sinclair and Tressell—pursues a line that finds almost no echo at all in psychoanalysis and its offshoots. While a materialist understanding of society was at the centre of uprising, war, murder (e.g. of Rosa Luxembourg) and the Russian revolution, the conceptually much more slippery mixture of interior 'psychic' mysteries and the magical power of the expert took root among a Western intelligentsia whom these huge events on the world stage appeared almost to pass by. With only a few minor setbacks in mid-twentieth century, this essentially idealist current flows unabated into the twenty-first.

It is not as if the swirling fashions of thought that made and make up this current are characterised by any noticeable unanimity: the principal psychological approaches, for example, spent and continue to spend many years in bitter dispute. Psychoanalysis, behaviourism, positivist 'science', 'humanistic' approaches of the mid-twentieth century such as those of Carl Rogers, Abraham Maslow, Fritz Perls and others, existentialism and phenomenology, plus the cognitivist, social constructionist and 'postmodernist' approaches of more recent times, may often seem to have very little in common, and have certainly fought hard to carve out their own distinctive territory. And yet at the centre of this quarrelsome mish-mash of ideas and practices is a gaping nothingness that, paradoxically, serves in one respect to unify them all. This is that *none* of them has anything to say about how the apparatus of power and interest that so clearly operates at the level of society comes to be reflected in the subjectivity of individuals—or even *whether* it does.

It is true, of course, that, until the capitulation of Eastern communism in the late 1980s, Marxism enjoyed a strong vogue in sociology and some other academic disciplines, and it is true too that some of Foucault's ideas took root (somewhat belatedly) in a rather far-flung corner of 'postmodernist' psychology; but all the same power and interest *as inescapable material factors* in the lives and minds of human beings (as opposed simply to features of 'discourse') have just not figured in psychological thinking. Such an oversight, I would argue, can only reflect the operation of repression on a massive scale.

In my view the effects of this repression can be observed at the most general, public level as well as in quite specific, private social exchanges. In popular culture, for example, the 'reasons' for events are nearly always sought in the conduct and intentions of individuals (usually in the form of 'blame'— see Chapter Four). This is largely an *interior* matter, i.e. a question of psychological causes originating in individuals' heads that have, so to speak, escaped out into the real world by way of their actions. Attempts to reverse the direction of this causation, so that individual's conduct is seen as *reactive to* events originating outside them, are likely to be seen as 'excuses'.

Explanations that take an exterior (from outside in) as opposed to an interior (from inside out) point of view are thus likely to evoke both incomprehension and disapproval. And it is precisely these reactions that one can often see on the faces of those to whom power and interest are offered as *explanatory* concepts in the course of private conversation. For example, when I have suggested to colleagues or students that Freud's retraction of the seduction hypothesis in favour of *fantasised* sexual abuse as the generator of 'hysteria' was a factor of his need to earn a living (see above), I have often felt that they have simply not been able to comprehend what I am saying, but see it as a kind of below-the-belt slur on Freud's character—rather as if I had uttered an obscenity so out of context that people couldn't be quite sure they'd heard it right. I've often had the same feeling when I've suggested to groups of professionals that therapists and counsellors (among whom, after all, I count myself) shy away from an explanation of our activities in terms of interest because it would seem to undermine our very *raison d'être*—i.e. it would undermine the 'scientific' rationale for our practice. This idea seems to be seen often not just as uncomfortable but as, literally, unthinkable. 'Yes, but what do you *mean* by interest?' people say, puzzlement written all over their faces; 'Could you *define* it?'

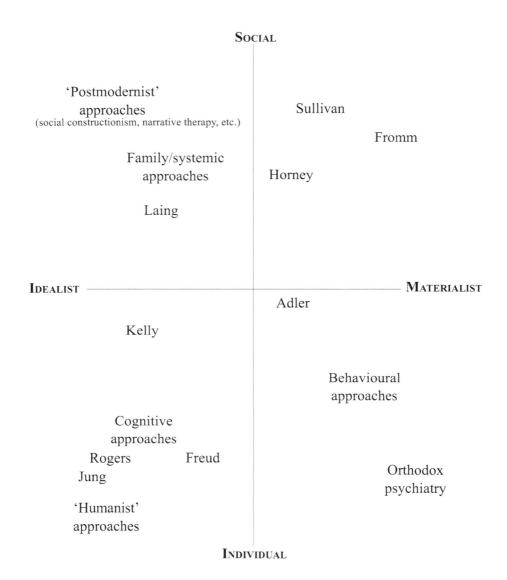

Figure 1.1 The conceptual space of therapy

In the world of twentieth-century therapeutic psychology, people do things because of impulses, intentions, cognitions or conditioned reflexes of which they may or may not be aware. This inevitably means that, at least implicitly, they are *responsible* for their actions and that change can be brought about only through some kind of *decision* on their part. Such decisions may not be easy, they may need to be based on 'insight' brought about by therapeutic interpretation or intervention; but when all is said and done, 'it's up to *you*'.

If we plot the principal approaches to psychotherapy along the axes 'idealist–materialist' and 'social–individual', as in Figure 1.1, it can be seen that only a very small proportion take cognisance of influences upon the subject that are both social and material, while pretty well all the conventional mainstream approaches cluster in the individual/idealist quadrant

The best name I can think of for the philosophy that underlies this phenomenon is 'magical voluntarism'. The central contention here is that, with perhaps the expert help of your therapist or counsellor, *you* can change the world *you* are in the last analysis responsible for, so that it no longer causes you distress. The way may certainly be hard, possibly (at the expensive end of the therapeutic spectrum) necessitating Odyssean ventures into the Unconscious, but ultimately salvation depends upon personal acts of will.

This was the principal achievement of the founders of modern psychotherapy: to turn the relation of person to world inside out, such that the former becomes the creator of the latter. With many 'postmodernist' approaches (e.g. 'narrative therapy') magical voluntarism reaches its apotheosis: the world is made of words, and if the story you find yourself in causes you distress, tell yourself another one.

From any rational, scientific standpoint, this kind of view is completely incoherent—indeed it is psychotic. And yet the universe of discourse in which it is put forward *is*, essentially, a rational, scientific one: the propositions of 'psychology' purport to be statements about our own nature and the nature of our world, and in this specific case it is asserted that our world is made of words and can be remade through rearranging words. That such a preposterous notion could be seriously put forward and maintained by people considered to be social scientists is inexplicable unless one introduces into the explanatory framework the notion of *interest*. In other words, it cannot be that the proposition in question is *true*; it can only be that it is *useful*, i.e. that it *suits the interests* both of those who assert it and those who assent to it. As long as consideration of interest is repressed we are likely to remain utterly mystified about the causes and cures of our psychological ills, trying instead to find our way in a make-believe world while looking for guidance principally to the adepts of magical voluntarism.

But once we make *interest* our focus, things become much clearer.

The stake counsellors and therapists have in maintaining an individualist and idealist account of emotional distress is obvious, for only such an account can legitimate the role of professional practitioner. Early in his career, Freud himself nearly stumbled into the dilemma posed for therapeutic practice by the realisation that psychological distress is in essence nothing more than unhappiness brought about by adverse circumstances. (His oft-quoted observation that 'neurotic misery' is merely the mask of 'common unhappiness' was made in 1895,[9] well before he had perfected the complex psychic apparatus that justified the professional practice of psychoanalysis.)

Clearly, any such insight as this points in a very different direction from that implied in the professional practice of therapy. A therapist can hope to act only upon the sufferer, and is in no position to act upon the sufferer's *world*. Therapeutic interest will therefore dictate that reasons for distress are found within, and not outside the person; if they are not, therapy will have to be abandoned (Freud, let it be noted, duly 'found' such reasons). Furthermore, not only must the causes of distress be both personal and interior, they must also be subject in one way or another to the influence of the therapist. At this point, I suggest, therapists find themselves uncomfortably close to magicians, and it is not surprising if the concepts and rituals of therapeutic cure (e.g. 'interpretation of the transference') bear a strong resemblance to the spells and incantations of sorcerers.

However, it is not just the interests of therapists that are in play here, but also the interests of their clients, as well as those of the wider society.

One has only to consider the typical ingredients of religious belief, or indeed the bulk of the output of Hollywood, to appreciate the fundamental appeal of magic to pretty well all of us. Reconciling ourselves to the harshness of life, the inevitability of death and the resistance of the world to our efforts to change it, are things none of us finds easy, and anything that promises to increase our personal power over fate can anticipate an enthusiastic reception from most of us. Our interest in there being accessible solutions to the troubles that beset us could scarcely be stronger, and any guru, therapist or celebrity who tells us we can do anything we want, overcome any obstacle, change ourselves from the inside out, is likely to get an attentive audience.

The alternative to magical voluntarism—e.g. that the world is unyielding to mere wishes, and must be worked upon in patient collaboration with others— is likely to get the thumbs down, and proponents of 'material realism' tend not to find themselves elevated to cult status at all quickly. For this is, in comparison, a somewhat bleak philosophy, recognising that even with blood, sweat and tears a good outcome is not assured, and that damage once done may well be irreparable. How much more attractive is the idea that a relatively brief association with a sorcerer, priest, astrologer or therapist can heal the wounds of the past or unleash a golden future, than that the conditions of our existence are to a great extent the outcome of material forces far beyond our personal control, historically unchangeable and with an uncertain future only amenable at best to the efforts of concerted, communal (*political*) effort.

Therapy, then—as has been abundantly demonstrated in recent years—is likely to be a popular option,[10] but it is not only to the interests of therapists and their clients that it appeals. Arguably, indeed, those who stand to benefit most from its underlying philosophy are those likely to feel themselves least in need of it. For if therapy offers a magical solution to the majority who suffer the world's cruelties, it also provides handy advice for them to be given by the minority who inflict them: suffering is to be lessened not by attacking social injustice, but rather by the *personal* readjustment of the disadvantaged themselves. Whether such readjustment is to be achieved through 'counselling' or through half-baked political philosophies such as 'communitarianism',[11] in which moral exhortation replaces practical help, the message is the same: wealth and privilege have nothing to do with a brutally unbalanced social system, but are available to all who achieve the right psychological balance and act 'responsibly'. It is surely no coincidence that the increasing disparities in wealth and power,[12] both within and between countries over the past twenty-five years or so, have been accompanied by an explosion in the advocacy and provision of therapies and political prescriptions that have magical voluntarism at their core.

It is, then, only by taking into account the networks of *interest* that glue society together that we can really understand the undoubted success of counselling and psychotherapy, which are otherwise empirically unsupported, philosophically incoherent and mutually contradictory.[13]

But there is another factor that we need to consider if a fair account is to be given of the rise of therapy, especially around the middle of the twentieth century, and how it was that many well-informed and well-intentioned people— particularly of course professionals in the field—embraced and defended the 'therapeutic ethos' with passion, and sometimes courage. For it would certainly be wrong of me to give the impression that therapists and counsellors themselves are nothing but a bunch of consciously self-interested charlatans out to exploit human weakness and legitimate social inequality. This would of course be to *psychologise* the account in exactly the way I am arguing against throughout : it is not that individuals *decide* to act in accordance with interest (theirs or others'), but rather that, not least because interest is repressed, they find themselves caught up in a system in ways they cannot fully understand and would—if they could understand it—undoubtedly deplore.

Those of us who applauded the mid-century challenges that the likes of Carl Rogers, George Kelly, Fritz Perls and 'existentialist' writers issued to orthodox psychiatry, psychoanalysis and behaviourism, no doubt did so because they introduced much less mechanistic, objectivist and inhumane accounts of personal distress. But what we didn't notice was that, even though there was a new emphasis on the importance of decent personal relationships—both within and outside therapy—as well as on exploring the individual's subjectivity, we were still stuck with the same model of therapist–patient 'treatment' in which 'change' would come *from within*, almost certainly greatly facilitated by some kind of 'intervention' on the therapist's part. In other words, though some principles of 'the treatment of mental illness' were hotly disputed, and some quite important gains made in terms of humanising 'the therapeutic relationship', the fundamental paradigm shifted not one iota: we were still dealing with an individual (now 'client' rather than 'patient') expected, with of course therapeutic help, to seek salvation through personal change. Furthermore, absolutely no progress had been made in reducing the confusion which inevitably flows from representing an interest-soaked enterprise as a scientific procedure—if anything, 'humanistic' approaches made things worse, as they introduced into therapeutic psychology ethical and aesthetic elements which are impossible to square with a model of dispassionate, professional advice.

The attack on the 'medical model' that coincided with the burgeoning of the new therapies was no doubt a reaction against the heartless scientism of psychiatry, orthodox psychoanalysis and 'behaviour therapy'. All of these, in their own way, claimed an objectivity and scientific validity that was in fact quite bogus. Patients were 'diagnosed' with 'illnesses' for which extraordinarily haphazard 'treatments' such as electro-convulsive therapy, insulin comas, brain surgery and drugs were prescribed; a minority might be subjected to the supposedly neutral, *technical* procedures of Freudian analysis; others would undergo the relatively newer, 'scientifically established' behavioural techniques based on the conditioned learning experiments of Pavlov and Skinner. In every case there was the same emphasis on the aloof indifference of the clinician to anything but the technical modification of 'symptoms', and almost no attention would be paid to the circumstances of patients' lives beyond the immediate family (and by no means always that); neither was any serious consideration given to the subjective experience of 'mental illness'.

Any critical and sensitive observer walking into almost any psychiatric institution in the 1950s would thus find him- or herself confronted with a population of bemused and desperate 'psychotic' and 'neurotic' patients, whose always disturbed and often devastating life circumstances simply didn't figure as causal elements in the theory and practice of those responsible for their care.

Hardly surprising, then, that so many of us embraced the new therapies with such enthusiasm: at least we could talk to patients as human beings about the issues that mattered to them and respond with compassion. But instead of developing a critique of the society that gave rise to our clients' difficulties, we replaced the dead scientism of conventional approaches with moralising critiques of individual development and theories about ideal human being. Instead of considering the material circumstances of people's lives, we got into 'relationships' and 'spirituality'. Whether followers of Carl Rogers, Fritz Perls, Eric Berne, Albert Ellis, George Kelly—or any other of the many therapeutic gurus who came to prominence in the second half of the twentieth century—the emphasis was always on what the *individual* should do to overcome or compensate for personal inadequacies of one kind or another.

Even though such inadequacies might be considered with (Rogerian) 'warmth, empathy, and genuineness' in a setting where the therapist made no attempt to hide behind a mask of cold impersonality, the onus nevertheless was always on the client to 'take responsibility' and make the necessary personal changes indicated by therapy.

In fact, this placed a new burden on people to whom life had already been less than kind. For failure to be 'cured' (not a term anyone used, but which nevertheless lurks at the heart of the whole idea of 'therapy') meant *personal* failure: either a moral failure of will (refusal to take responsibility) or falling short as a human being (failure to reach the aesthetic standards set up by, for instance, such arbiters of 'self-actualisation' as Abraham Maslow and Fritz Perls). If the scientific pretensions of the 'old treatments' resulted in a frightening impersonality and neglect of subjectivity, at least they didn't (intentionally) tamper with your soul; in contrast, the new therapies assigned themselves a scope more characteristic of religion than science and, at least tacitly, invested themselves with an authority that went well beyond the objective and technical.

Margaret Thatcher's much-cited view that 'There's no such thing as society, only individuals and their families,' finds an unacknowledged echo in almost all approaches to therapy, including those that continued throughout the second half of the twentieth century to wrap themselves in the mantle of 'science'. For example, in asserting its claim to 'evidence-based' credibility, 'cognitive behaviour therapy' (CBT) takes no more note of social influences in the generation of distress than do the 'humanistic' therapies.

CBT—in fact more a kind of rhetorical construction than a serious, theory-based practice—is perhaps the least convincing of all therapies from the standpoint of a critical onlooker. In combining the 'scientific rigour' of behaviourism with the mentalism of, essentially, popular psychology, CBT is par excellence the product of professional interest; it appeals to common-sense ideas of how people do things (action follows deliberation) while attempting to preserve the technical mystique that behaviourism managed to establish within academic psychology precisely on the grounds of *anti*-mentalism. This opportunistic marriage of incompatible approaches is then supported by its doctors through the judicious highlighting of a handful of research studies from the huge, chaotic and contradictory literature[14] that has developed in the psychotherapy field over the past fifty years or so.

In some ways the concessions made by behaviour therapists to 'cognitive' factors, in order to give birth to the more 'credible' hybrid CBT, is paralleled by the development of 'postmodernist' approaches in therapy (and indeed psychology more generally), in which the implausible constraints imposed by a too-rigid scientism yield to a framework more generously accommodating of the needs of the therapy market.

There is no doubt that many dissenters from the ruling positivist/ behaviourist line suffered under its domination, undergoing years of frustration as they struggled in vain to get a hearing for therapeutic approaches that paid proper respect to subjectivity. For some, the advent of 'postmodernism' seemed to provide exactly the breakthrough they had longed for, ushering in a 'new paradigm'[15] that would at last allow an unfettered exploration of crucial therapeutic issues. But, I think, one only needed to step for a moment outside the consulting room to see that this was not so much a new dawn of reflective insight and intellectual tolerance as a *deregulation* of the academic and therapeutic orthodoxies. The coming of postmodernism had more to do with market expansion than with progress of psychological understanding.

Although it is quite common for academic psychologists as well as therapists to feel that they are still fighting old battles, in fact there is no longer much sign either in academia or the wider culture of the dominance of rigid scientism. The final two decades of the twentieth century saw a relaxation of control in which, for example, psychoanalysis emerged from long years of scornful neglect and dismissal, 'alternative' forms of medicine and therapy suddenly found themselves flourishing, and 'blue sky' thinking could all but pass for research. Academic psychologists could discuss 'grounded theory', 'action' and 'qualitative' research, 'discourse analysis' and other forms of uncontrolled and even speculative investigation in ways that would have been unthinkable only a short while before. Philosophers expressed their contempt for any notion such as 'truth' or 'right' that was not translated into a kind of linguistic illusion (Derrida[16]) or the pragmatic construction of a particular self-interested group (Rorty, [17] MacIntyre[18]). At the same time, university provision expanded dramatically (interestingly, in Britain, mainly through a simple re-branding of other already existing educational facilities) and with it the provision of counselling courses of every hue. The direction of pretty well all public institutions, including of course education and health, became subject to a uniform Business culture.

Business is instinctively antipathetic to the 'old' academic values of scholarship, intellectual rigour and the disinterested search for truth, which in fact not only do not facilitate, but actually stand in the way of market expansion and money making. Many of those working in health and education thus found themselves completely disorientated and bemused as the crass 'philosophies' and 'techniques' of business management suddenly came to be imposed on them from the highest levels of their organisations. The conceptual flaccidity and generously inclusive nature of 'postmodernism' was ideally suited as an underlying rationale for creating and running new markets where what mattered was 'wealth creation' and not critically rigorous thought.[19]

What we witnessed, I would argue, was not the tortured, hard-won emergence of a new paradigm, but the (counter-revolutionary) imposition of a 'new' orthodoxy. Orthodoxies are about power, not truth, which perhaps is why for many of us the changes that overcame our places of work had an uncomfortably familiar feel about them: the message might seem different but the medium was the same, and in fact our freedom to think independently about our discipline and to develop our practice creatively was greatly curtailed—not, as before, by a kind of doctrinal bullying, but by the deliberate application of (non-professional) managerial control.

Thus, although *markets* were deregulated, control of production was not, and the new managerial classes, blindly responsive to the interests of neo-liberal capitalism, were assiduous in making sure that, at least as they saw it, all business-unfriendly practices were eradicated from professional and academic institutions, and procedures of discipline and surveillance were introduced into middle-class occupations that formerly had been applied only to workers. Although in the clinical field 'quality' was supposedly 'assured' through the establishment of 'tough targets', 'evidence-based practice' and 'clinical governance', etc., the managers' visceral hostility to knowledge, combined with their unawareness of their own ignorance, meant that in fact the field quickly became an incoherent collage of ideas and practices whose only common feature was a superficial market credibility. But that, of course, was all that mattered.

In this way, the turning of the millennium marked no great progress in psychological understanding, but rather, compared with what had existed only a few years before, an enormous expansion in the market for counselling and therapy. No longer constrained by a 'medical model' to limit their attentions to the manifestation of a handful of 'neuroses', therapists and counsellors are now able to claim as their legitimate province huge swathes of human conduct[20] ranging from grief to criminality, family discord to international conflict.

The fact that this individualist/idealist bandwagon rolls on so successfully is testament to how little truth matters in this sphere (as in so many others). Magical voluntarism may be difficult to support rationally, but it pays, and at a time in history when the 'bottom line' is—not for the first time—paramount, we are unlikely to see any diminution in its sway.

This is not to say, however, that the individualism and idealism of orthodox approaches to psychotherapy have not had their critics, right throughout the period we have been considering. The world-view implicit in Freudian psychoanalysis is so bizarre[21] that it is not surprising that from the very beginnings of modern psychotherapy rational sympathisers found it impossible to swallow whole.

For example, even though still focused very much on the individual, Alfred Adler soon left the camp Freud was endeavouring to set up because he was unable to overlook the fact that our place in *society* is just about our most fundamental concern from a psychological point of view. Subsequent apostates from orthodox psychoanalysis in the first half of the twentieth century included the once-familiar trio of Erich Fromm, Karen Horney and Harry S. Sullivan,[22] all of whom placed great emphasis on the ways in which we are social products whose distress can neither be understood nor fully dealt with if divorced from its social context. Although prominent and even influential around mid-century, their perspective did not take permanent hold in the field (students of clinical psychology these days are quite likely not to have heard of them). A more recent proponent of a social perspective within psychiatric disorder (notably 'schizophrenia'), coupled with a subtle and profound consideration of subjectivity, was of course R.D. Laing.[23] Briefly influential, as with the others, Laing's work seems now to be regarded more as a kind of 'typical' sixties extravagance than an important contribution to our understanding of serious distress.

The 'therapeutic community' movement, at its peak (in Britain) in the 1960s constituted an attempt to take social factors into account in the treatment of 'mental illness', such that several previously conventional psychiatric institutions were transformed into mini-societies in which the chief therapeutic focus was on how the inmates—patients and staff—related to each other. While this represented a laudable attempt to get beyond 'individuals and their families', the project foundered (among other reasons) because of the inevitable insularity of the communities themselves: as it does with individual therapy, the world that had originally generated patients' difficulties lay in wait beyond the hospital doors to re-inflict its injuries once they were discharged. (Asylum would indeed be the 'treatment of choice' for most forms of psychological distress were it not for its impermanence.)

More recently, the development of 'community psychology'[24] as an off-shoot of clinical psychology reflects (and contributes to) an awareness of the issues raised above and tries to counter the insulating effects of 'treatment' by extending its influence into the actual communities in which people live. In this way 'community psychologists' and other community workers may try to help people tackle some of the noxious features of their social environment that are amenable to communal action, involving if they can those powers within the community (local authorities, etc.) that bear responsibility for them. At this point the role of psychologist or community worker begins to shade into that of politician, and what the implications of this might be is not clear, but in any case it does in my view reflect a more accurate appreciation of the causes of distress than just about any other 'clinical' discipline.

All these forms of practical dissent within psychoanalysis, psychiatry and clinical psychology constitute an at least implicit critique of magical voluntarism, and attempt to take social factors seriously. In parallel with, but not necessarily allied to them, there has since mid-twentieth century been a constant stream of criticism both of the conceptual foundations of conventional therapies as well as of the inadequacy of evidence of their effectiveness. The motives of such critics—ranging from H.J. Eysenck in clinical psychology and Thomas Szasz in psychiatry to more recent writers such as Robert Fancher,[25] William Epstein[26] and Donald Eisner[27]—have varied considerably, but they represent a very large body of opinion that questions the soundness of the very basis of therapeutic psychology.

At an even broader conceptual level have been the critiques such as those of Michel Foucault[28] and Christopher Lasch[29] of the whole apparatus of 'treatment', seeing them as the result of an essentially *disciplinary* political exercise. This kind of critique has laid the foundations for a widespread awareness of the social consequences—indeed the socio-economic and socio-political aims—of an ideology of 'therapy' which is closely allied to the interests of corporate capitalism.[30]

Though not focally 'therapeutic', the 'critical theory' developed throughout much of the twentieth century by thinkers and researchers of the Frankfurt School of social criticism, essentially Marxist in its approach, probably constitutes the most thoroughgoing and intellectually challenging attempt to focus on the societal origins of individual malaise. Herbert Marcuse's *One Dimensional Man,*[31] for example, offers a brilliantly powerful demonstration of late capitalism's crippling effect on our subjectivity, while Jürgen Habermas has worked assiduously over the years (and in my view with great success) to rescue truth from the postmodernists.[32] Russell Jacoby's *Social Amnesia*[33] is an appreciative account of the Frankfurt thinkers' assault on the social blindness and individualism of much mainstream philosophical and psychological writing.

However, I find it puzzling—even paradoxical—that so many of the Frankfurt writers, in order to theorise the influence of material, societal conditions on personal subjectivity, felt it necessary to turn for help to psychoanalysis. The attempt to marry Marxism and psychoanalysis was of course encountered more or less from the outset in the writings of left-wing Freudians such as Reich and Fenichel and is found more recently in the work of a range of more directly therapeutic writers (e.g. Joel Kovel;[34] the British therapists grouped around the journal *Free Associations*), much of whose work deserves respectful attention. But the union of Marx and Freud seems to me to be so strained as to be unsustainable. The basic argument (as put, for example, by Jacoby) seems to be that in psychoanalysis Freud posits an (essentially pessimistic) view of the human psyche as shaped culturally and historically by forces beyond the reach of the individual's autonomous control. While that may superficially point to some common ground between Freud and Marx, the fundamental differences seem to me overwhelming. What can be gleaned from his writings of Freud's political views is more typical of the saloon bar than of dialectical materialism, and though certainly Freud refers to himself on occasion as a 'revolutionary', this is certainly meant in an intellectual rather than a political sense. Jacoby states the case well (and, somewhat strangely, cuts the ground from under his own feet):

> Psychologism is the constitutional failing of psychology, *psychoanalysis included*. Social process and conflicts are read as psychological and individual ones. Society is conceived as simply an individual or psychological pact between men, not as a piece of reality with its own social gravity. (*op. cit.*, p. 65, my italics)

No matter how intelligent and accurate critiques of the therapeutic orthodoxy have been, they have been dealt with easily enough by the rhetorical devices of the ruling magical-voluntarist orthodoxy. This would of course be puzzling if the debate were truly the scientific one it pretends to be, but in fact even at its most sharply divided, any argument between idealist/individualists on the one hand and social materialists on the other is almost bound to be vacuous because, once again, the criterion of validity is not truth, but power.[35] Virtually all the critics of the orthodoxy, however impeccable their credentials, have sooner or later been marginalised not because their arguments are untrue, but because they are inconvenient.

If the world we live in were really constructed of 'discourse' none of this would matter very much, and 'reality' would change shape and colour according to the flow of power and interest. The success of 'spin' and the apparent absence of any serious consequences of our cavalier treatment of old notions such as right and truth might suggest that we can indeed get along very well without pursuing these 'grand narratives' of the Enlightenment. Alternatively (which is my view), it may be that our indifference to material reality leads to an increasingly depleted environment, unbalanced society and tortured subjectivity. The last of these three—and the one with which this book is of course principally concerned—is a function very largely of the first two, and to understand how we come to suffer avoidable psychological distress we are going to have to extend our gaze beyond the 'inner worlds' of individuals to take account not only of social structure, but also of the limitations placed on our imaginings by the real world.

As far as mainstream approaches are concerned, our understanding of psychological distress has advanced over the past century hardly at all—arguably, it has even regressed. Without quite fundamental changes in the tools of our self-analysis—most obviously the lifting of our repression of interest—there is no guarantee that we'll do any better in the new millennium.

Notes

1. An excellent all-round account of the development of therapeutic psychology and its current status can be found in Dilys Davies, 1997. *Counselling in Psychological Services*. Open University Press.

2. See for example Andrew Samuels, 2001. *Politics on the Couch*. Profile Books.

3. Masson, J.M. (ed). 1985. *The Complete Letters of Sigmund Freud to Wilhelm Fliess 1887–1904*. Cambridge, MA. and London: Harvard University Press.

4. Much of the following discussion is formerly published in Smail, D. 1995. Power and the origins of unhappiness: working with individuals. *Journal of Community and Applied Social Psychology*, *5*, 347–56.

5. My emphasis in this and following quotations.

6. Masson, J.M. 1985. *The Assault on Truth*. Harmondsworth: Penguin Books.

7. S. Freud, 1915. *Standard Edition of the Complete Psychological Works*. Trans. and ed. James Strachey, Vol. XIV, p. 201. London: Hogarth:

> We now seem to know all at once what the difference is between a conscious and an unconscious presentation. The two are not, as we supposed, different registrations of the same content in different psychical localities, nor yet different functional states of cathexis in the same locality; but the conscious presentation comprises the presentation of the thing plus the presentation of the word belonging to it, while the unconscious presentation is the presentation of the thing alone… Now, too, we are in a position to state precisely what it is the repression denies to the rejected presentation in the transference neuroses: what it denies to the presentation is translation into words which shall remain attached to the object. A presentation which is not put into words, or a psychical act which is not hypercathected, remains thereafter in the Ucs in a state of repression.

8. For a brilliant study of aspects of Freud's political and cultural background, see Carl E. Schorske, 1981 (originally 1961). *Fin-de-Siècle Vienna*. Cambridge University Press.

9. S. Freud and J. Breuer. *Studies on Hysteria*. Penguin edition, 1974, p. 393.

10. For a powerful critique of the psychology industry see Tana Dineen, 1999. *Manufacturing Victims*. London: Constable.

11. For a particularly crass exposition of this 'movement' see Amitai Etzioni, 1995. *The Spirit of Community*. Fontana.

12. See, for example, Richard G. Wilkinson, 1996. *Unhealthy Societies*. Routledge.

13. This proposition will, I know, strike many as contentious. The best single source I can think of to cite in its support—even if only indirectly—is Colin Feltham (ed.): *Controversies in Psychotherapy and Counselling*, Sage Publications, 1999.

14. Some of the nature of this is conveyed in the excellent volume edited by Windy Dryden and Colin Feltham, 1992. *Psychotherapy and its Discontents*. Open University Press.

15. See Richard House, 2003. *Therapy Beyond Modernity*. Karnac.

16. See Christopher Norris, 1987. *Derrida*. Fontana Modern Masters.

17. Richard Rorty, 1980. *Philosophy and the Mirror of Nature*. Blackwell.

18. Alasdair MacIntyre, 1981. *After Virtue*. Duckworth.

19. For an excellent critique see Greg Philo and David Miller, 2001. *Market Killing*. Longman.

20. A number of critics have lined up against this tendency. See for example Tana Dineen, *op.cit.*; Susan Hansen, Alec McHoul and Mark Rapley, 2003. *Beyond Help*, PCCS Books; Frank Furedi, 2003. *Therapy Culture: Cultivating vulnerability in an anxious age*, Routledge; Vanessa Pupavac, 2004. Psychosocial interventions and the demoralisation of humanitarianism. *Journal of biosocial Science*, *36*, 491–504.

21. Freud has, of course, not been short of critics. The two best that I know are Ernest Gellner, 1985. *The Psychoanalytic Movement*, Paladin; and Richard Webster, 1995. *Why Freud Was Wrong*. HarperCollins.

22. Works by these writers are too numerous to cite. I have listed the most important on my website at www.davidsmail.freeuk.com/psypsy.htm

23. See, for example, R.D. Laing, 1967. *The Politics of Experience and the Bird of Paradise*. Penguin.

24. A good account is to be found in Jim Orford, 1992. *Community Psychology: Theory and Practice*. Wiley.

25. Robert T. Fancher, 1995. *Cultures of Healing*. W.H. Freeman.

26. William M. Epstein, 1995. *The Illusion of Psychotherapy*. Transaction Publishers.

27. Donald A. Eisner, 2000. *The Death of Psychotherapy*. Praeger.

28. Michel Foucault, 1979. *Discipline and Punish*. Harmondsworth: Penguin Books.

29. Christopher Lasch, 1985. *The Minimal Self: Psychic survival in troubled times*. Pan Books.

30. See, again, the works of Dineen; Hansen *et al.*; and Furedi—all cited above.

31. Herbert Marcuse, 1964. *One-Dimensional Man*. Beacon Press.

32. See, for example, Jürgen Habermas, 1987. *The Philosophical Discourse of Modernity*. Polity Press.

33. Russell Jacoby, 1975. *Social Amnesia: A critique of conformist psychology from Adler to Laing*. Harvester.

34. See, for example, Joel Kovel, 1983. *Against the State of Nuclear Terror*. Pan.

35. Just how vacuous the argument can be may be judged from an examination, once again, of the contributions to Colin Feltham's (ed.) *Controversies in Psychotherapy and Counselling*, cited above, in which quite often the *same* research evidence is cited to support fundamentally opposed views.

2

A Societal Perspective

In the course of this chapter I shall suggest a number of things that many people find very hard to accept. For example:

- The best way of understanding ourselves and the significance of our actions is not through personal reflection and introspection, (i.e. we have as individuals no privileged access to our own motives).
- Most of the time we personally have very little control over our actions (e.g., 'cognition' does not control action).
- There is no such thing as will-power.
- The societal operation of power and interest is immeasurably more important in understanding human conduct than are the components of personal 'psychology'.

Why such propositions are hard to accept is, I believe, because they appear to fly in the face not only of the orthodox tenets of 'official' psychology, but because they seem also to contradict our common-sense experience of ourselves. For when we look inside ourselves, we all tend to 'discover' exactly those phenomena that traditionally form the chapter-headings of psychology text books, i.e. feelings, thoughts, perceptions, intentions, etc., etc. From this experience, backed by academic authority, we are almost bound to conclude that, as individuals, we harbour systems of sensation, emotion, cognition and will which, in their various combinations, will be sufficient to explain our 'behaviour'. To understand why this common-sense experience could be misleading, we need first to consider how it is arrived at.

Each one of us occupies, in the grander scheme of things, an infinitesimal space for an infinitesimal length of time; and yet, for us as individuals, this is all the space and all the time we have, and so it appears subjectively hugely significant.

Our greatest intimacy is with the bodily sensations that mediate our relations with the world around us: because we *feel*, physically, what is going on, we have a sense of 'interiority' which seems to be just about the most indubitable indication of what is happening to us. We feel we know what is going on in our own 'minds' with an especially privileged certainty, while we can make only educated guesses about what goes on in the minds of others. The physical experience of doing things—experience which is absolutely unavoidable—convinces us that, most of the time, 'doing things' is the upshot of internal processes like assessing options and taking decisions. We seem thus to be given an indisputable knowledge of wishes and intentions which are entirely private to ourselves, and our greatest guarantee of the truth of someone else's wishes and intentions seems therefore to be to induce them to give a truthful account of them from their own inner experience.

Our understanding and assessment of the world around us is mediated by the people and things we come into direct, bodily contact with. The language we speak we learn from those who speak to us, and we speak (extraordinarily precisely) with their cadences and their accent. Our experience of social power is transmitted by those with whom we have daily contact—first families, then educators, then employers (and of course the social networks in which these are embedded). On the whole, the nearer people and things are to us the more significance we are likely to accord to their effect upon us (inevitably, for example, children experience their parents as enormously powerful). At the same time we are, of course, surrounded by a complex apparatus conveying information and controlling meaning. The extent to which we are able to penetrate this apparatus will determine our understanding of our world. In all these spheres we are, as individuals, surrounded by an horizon beyond which the world is a mystery.

From the perspective of time also we occupy a life-span which gives us a sense of the 'length' of history. The elderly live in an era which, beyond the personal reach of younger people, becomes merely a realm of nostalgia. The Norman Conquest seems to most of us (who know about it at all) to belong deep in the mists of the past—and yet there are still families living on estates seized then, and it takes only 13 seventy-year-olds, living back-to-back, to get there.

We live, then, at the centre of a world of 'proximal space-time', a world experienced from the self-as-centre.

Just as it was difficult for mediæval men and women to shake off the conviction—so powerfully endorsed by their own senses—that the earth was at the centre of the universe, so does it appear self-evident to us that it is our experience as individuals embodied in time and space which yields us our most reliable knowledge of how we and others tick. It is my belief that we are as profoundly misled by the perspective from self-as-centre as our ancestors were by their geocentric view of the universe.

Among my reasons for doubting the adequacy of this view is my observation, over many years' practice as a clinical psychologist, that conventional therapeutic theories fail to account for the ways in which psychological distress comes about and seriously misrepresent the extent to which it can be alleviated. Indeed, the term 'psychological' distress is itself a misnomer, since it dislocates and disembodies distress, pushing it into a realm of ideality where it loses all ties with material reality.

Table 2.1 summarises some of the principal ways in which clinical practice tends not to support clinical theory.

THEORY SUGGESTS	CLINICAL EXPERIENCE TEACHES
Insight leads to change	We are not in control of our conduct; therapeutic change is not demonstrable
People may 'assume responsibility'	There is no such thing as 'will-power'
Thought ('cognitions') leads to action ('behaviour')	The causes of our conduct are frequently mysterious, and rationally unalterable
Characteristics/actions (real or imagined) of the therapist are central to change (e.g. 'transference'; 'warmth, empathy and genuineness'; behavioural and/or cognitive manipulations, etc.)	People's conduct is controlled by more potent influences in their social environment

Table 2.1 Theory–practice conflict

Just about every brand of therapy works—explicitly or tacitly—on the assumption that the revelation of people's (undesirable, mistaken or counter-productive) motives will lead either directly or indirectly to their being able to change to more appropriate conduct. A central theme of any 'talking cure' is *why* clients feel and act as they do, the aim of course being to replace, through insight, the bad reasons that lead to 'dysfunctional' conduct with good reasons that lead to 'change'. Once people 'see' where they've gone wrong, it is assumed, they will be able to switch seamlessly to a more rewarding set of 'behaviours'.

In practice, however, things are not half so easy. It is not uncommon for people to have a pretty good idea of how they have come to feel as they do even before they start therapy or counselling, but even where the procedures (as they often do) clarify the background quite successfully, it is still very frequently the case that 'change' is as stubbornly hard to achieve as ever.

Nothing exposes the technical shortcomings of therapy as clearly as the observation that simply providing people with an accurate account (or 'interpretation') of the reasons for their difficulties is not enough to bring about improvement. In the early days of therapy it was hoped that the disappointing inadequacy of 'intellectual insight' would be corrected by a more powerful experience of 'emotional insight', but here again even the most epiphanic experiences guarantee no greater or more fundamental changes in conduct.

At this point all pretence of therapy as a technology of change is abandoned and, more or less overtly, moralism in one form or another takes the stage. Even though therapists recognise the futility of exhorting their clients to exercise will-power, some such concept necessarily lies at the heart of notions such as 'resistance' which are invoked to account for people's failure to profit from insight. It is thus recognised that for 'insight' to be effective it must be combined with 'responsibility'. Clients must undertake the responsibility of exercising their will to change. If they do not, they court the danger of acquiring the diagnosis of 'inadequate personality'.

This whole model is, of course, unquestioningly rationalist, and assumes throughout that our conduct is based upon consciously or unconsciously chosen personal strategies. (That such strategies might be unconsciously chosen does not compromise their rationality; it simply pushes it to another 'mental' level.) This rationalism is most clearly expressed in those therapies having an avowedly 'cognitivist' element, in which 'cognitions', 'beliefs' and 'attitudes', etc., are conceived as the generative elements of our conduct.

Here again, however, clinical experience is recalcitrant: while it is certainly possible for anyone (especially with the enthusiastic help of a therapist) to construct a coherent story about the mental origins of their feelings and actions, such stories frequently carry little conviction, and as often as not genuine puzzlement seems the more authentic attitude. Again, even where a rationalist explanation seems thoroughly plausible to both client and therapist, it is frustratingly often the case that this makes absolutely no difference to the former's ability to start doing things better, struggle though s/he might to do so.

Perhaps the most disturbing thing of all about clinical experience is the recurring lesson it teaches of therapeutic impotence. At first, usually, the very opposite seems to be the case, and everything the therapist hoped about his or her curative powers seems to be justified by the client's initial response to treatment: people who have perhaps never before been able to offload their deepest fears and anxieties about themselves positively bloom in the warmth and safety of the consulting room. Unfortunately, however, such initial gains tend not to last, and only a few sessions later the therapist may start to worry that he or she is after all not doing things quite right: the client starts to raise old complaints, and problems that seemed to have disappeared almost magically are again firmly back on the agenda. Rather like tender plants that thrive only in a greenhouse, it seems that people find that there is still a cold and hostile world waiting for them at the end of their therapy sessions—with, still, an overwhelmingly powerful grip upon them.

This mismatch between theory and practice has, I believe, a fairly obvious explanation, which is that in the case of psychotherapy the proper relation of theory to practice has been reversed: rather than theory arising out of experience (i.e. observation of what actually happens in the world), it has in fact been dictated by the *practical interests* of therapy.

In this way the left-hand column of Table 2.1 can best be understood as a list of circumstances that *need to be the case* if the interests of psychotherapy as professional practice are to be met. For therapeutic practice to be justifiable, the protagonists must necessarily be engaged in an essentially rational interchange in which the client is able to adjust his or her conduct in accordance with therapeutic influence, and the therapist must be in possession of either the techniques or the personal characteristics that mediate such influence effectively. Given this set of requirements, the theory obviously makes sense. The trouble is that the legitimate criterion of theoretical accuracy should not be the satisfaction of professional interest, but the adequacy of client response to treatment.

In order to re-establish a proper relationship between theory and practice we need, then, to allow practice to dictate theory; that is, to switch the columns of the table such that our theoretical speculations are *derived from* practical

CLINICAL EXPERIENCE TEACHES	THEORETICAL REQUIREMENTS
We are not in control of our conduct; therapeutic change is not demonstrable	Need to identify the causes of conduct *beyond* personal agency. These are likely to be biological as well as social
There is no such thing as 'will-power'	Need to establish the limits of 'responsibility'; factors that make free action possible
The causes of our conduct are frequently mysterious, and rationally unalterable	Rationalist explanations are insufficient; need to account for the disjunction between conduct and the accounts we give of it
People's conduct is controlled by more potent influences in their social environment	Need to develop a multi-layered understanding of *influence* (including therapeutic influence), its modes of operation and the reasons for the permanence/impermanence of its effects

Table 2.2 Experience generates theory

experience. This is, of course, not to imply that theoretical principles so derived would necessarily be accurate, but they would potentially at least be genuinely testable. Table 2.2 outlines how this revised relation between practice and theory might look.

In comparison with Table 2.1, the effect of Table 2.2 is to remove professional interest from the equation, and this makes it in some ways feel less controversial: it is easier for therapists to assent to the relations between practice and theory as set out in Table 2.2 without feeling a threat to their *raison d'être*, whereas the effect of Table 2.1 is to draw attention to the dissonances caused by interest.

If, then, we are to account adequately for the phenomena of distress (and for the inability of therapy to provide anything like a full treatment of them), we will need a theoretical structure that extends beyond the narrow confines of the consulting room, *relocating* both clients and therapists in the wider social world. In addition, if we are to be able to understand the obstinate resistance of 'symptoms' to 'treatment', we will need to *re-embody* clients as well as relocate them.

Figure 2.1 tries to summarise the implications for theory of the issues raised above and in Chapter One. The fundamental aim to is to suggest how the impress of social power works on the individual embodied subject to bring about the kind of 'clinical' distress that is familiar to practitioners (not to mention all the rest of us). There is of course a considerable risk that, if taken too literally, such diagrams as this can do more harm than good. For example, the separation between environment and person represented by the horizontal line is entirely artificial, since in reality there is no such separation: all of us are *within* the environment, and form part of it. However, I hope that the following commentary may help to avoid some of the possibly misleading aspects of Figure 2.1.

The person exists as an embodied being in a material environment that is structured both physically and (more important for our purposes) socially. The principal dynamic of social structure is *power*, which is transmitted through *interest* (see below). The most powerful influences that end up impinging upon the individual tend to be those furthest from him/her, i.e. economic, political and cultural powers, etc. These are mediated by lesser powers closer to the individual, ultimately via other individuals encountered in families, social groups, workplaces, etc.

The person is related to the environment physically, i.e. via his/her bodily constitution, which is subjectively experienced and expressed by him or her as feelings, dispositions, impulses, etc. Thus the world is impressed upon us *bodily*, and insofar as we are able to act back upon the world ('agency'), it cannot be done without the physical (embodied) activity of the subject, or of the subject in collaboration with others.

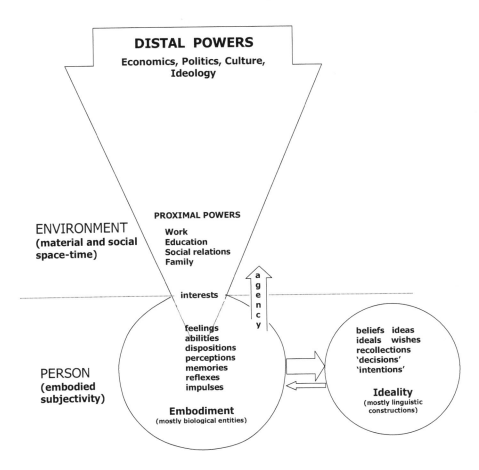

Figure 2.1 The Impress of Power

We represent our physical interaction with the environment through the use of ideas and concepts which, inevitably, are derived through language (see below). We struggle to articulate our feelings, impulses, memories, perceptions, etc., in linguistic forms that describe them as accurately as possible, and we conceptualise much of our embodied experience in terms that tend to take on a life of their own: 'beliefs', 'intentions', 'decisions', etc. This, I suggest, is best understood as a sphere of 'ideality' that, while it may have some influence on our embodied subjectivity (represented by the narrower arrow in Figure 2.1), has much less influence than it often seems, and is shaped by the embodied experience that underlies it (broader arrow) to a much greater extent than we tend to realise. It is with the sphere of ideality that traditional therapeutic psychology has mainly concerned itself, and as a consequence has become lost in a magical realm which in fact has no chance of impacting upon the real world of material space-time. Thus what we take to be 'psychology' in this respect *hypostatises* an immaterial world based on linguistic constructions, inevitably giving rise to a mythology of magical voluntarism that is, though highly plausible, doomed to impotence.

Power

Power, which may be defined broadly as the means of obtaining security or advantage, is, as already indicated, the fundamental dynamic of social structure. In other words, it is what shapes and maintains a society that forms, from our current Western perspective, a pyramidal hierarchy, at the peak of which is a small corporate plutocracy and at the bottom of which is a vast, largely politically atomised collectivity of consumers (the traditional working class of industrialised Western countries having been fractured and to a considerable extent exported to other parts of the globe). Distributed through the middle ranges are diminishing numbers of public-service workers and professionals, and an expanding bureaucracy of managers of various grades.

Table 2.3 summarises the principal kinds of power that operate within social space-time.

Biological Coercive	Embodied, very proximal but subjectively dominating.
Legal Economic Ideological (control of meaning, language, perspective and horizon)	Operate at variable distance in social space-time, ranging from the personal to the institutional; degree of influence and subjective prominence tend to be negatively correlated.

Table 2.3 Forms of power

As individuals, the form of power most readily available to us—'biological' power—is also the most limited in scope. For example, sheer muscle may loom large on the playground, in dysfunctional families and minor criminal sub-cultures, but as a means of influencing events in the wider world is likely to be counterproductive, and likely also to bring the individual into confrontation with coercive powers which most law-abiding citizens are otherwise unlikely to encounter. Physical attractiveness is another kind of biological power that is highly sought after, not to say greatly agonised over, by vast swathes of the population and serves as one of the principal engines of consumerism. (In this respect it is not a 'pure' form of biological power, but is heavily exploited and distorted by the advertising, public relations and entertainment industries.) On its own, however, beauty is a limited means of influence, and in fact probably launches few ships.

While education, social position and wealth may provide individuals with varying degrees of influence within their proximal world (including those forms of non-economic 'capital' that Pierre Bourdieu's work illumines so brightly),[1] the main hope for ordinary people of exercising power is to do so in cooperation with others (solidarity). Otherwise, coercive and legal powers are very much matters of state, while in the modern world economic and ideological powers operate beyond as well as within national boundaries, forming some of the most potent but least visible influences on our lives.

The control of meaning (ideological power) is of course an immensely important aspect of social control. The degree to which people can analyse and understand their situation and the influences that shape it depends upon their access to knowledge and information that exist largely in organisations and institutions which tend to have an interest in keeping them to themselves. The mass media of news and entertainment, again semi-independent of national control, constitute an enormous influence on our lives, and they are clearly about much more than simply the provision of objective information and innocent cultural stimulation and fun. The actual interests they serve are, however, largely opaque to the mass of their consumers.

It is important to note that the exercise of power is not simply malign. Partly, I suspect, because of our repression of interest and partly because of our observation of its well-known corrupting effects, we tend to think of the intrusion of power into our relations with each other as inevitably bad. And yet to *exclude* power from our social relations would be extraordinarily difficult. Indeed, it would be impossible. Loving relations between people are as dependent on the exercise of power as is the most brutal oppression—the difference is that benign power is exercised in the interest of its object (the 'other'), while malign power is exercised in the interest of the oppressor. The necessity of benign power is particularly obvious in the case of parent and child, but is also a significant factor in most of our personal relations, as well as in more formal relations (where successful) including, for example, those of teacher–pupil, employer–employee, and (not least) therapist–patient.

Proximal relations

It is not surprising that therapeutic conversations tend to focus almost exclusively on the client's proximal relations, particularly of course within the family, since it is these that loom largest in our everyday experience. So many of our joys and frustrations, loves and hatreds arise from our contact with those immediately around us that we can easily forget that there is a world beyond them which may in fact shift the level of explanation for their conduct beyond merely the desires and intentions that they seem to embody. The language of will and responsibility, decision and obstinacy, malice and generosity, and so on, that gives form to our reflections about what people do to us and we to them, seems entirely appropriate in the context of normal life, and indeed is taken over barely modified into the theoretical language of therapy. It is hard to resist being misled by this superficial plausibility of vocabulary.

Figure 2.2 attempts to represent the power relations within a stereotypical family of four, the thickness of the arrows indicating the potency of the influences involved. Almost anyone's proximal world is of course much more complex than this, but one can already see that, in accounting for any individual's conduct, a good deal more is in play than the simple autonomy of those involved. Furthermore, the interpersonal relations that directly influence the family members, including those stemming from their social and working worlds, are set in an infinitely wider field of power relations of which the individuals themselves need have no awareness. The limits of any single person's influence will depend on the power available to them, and beyond family and friends this may be very little indeed. For example, while the father's

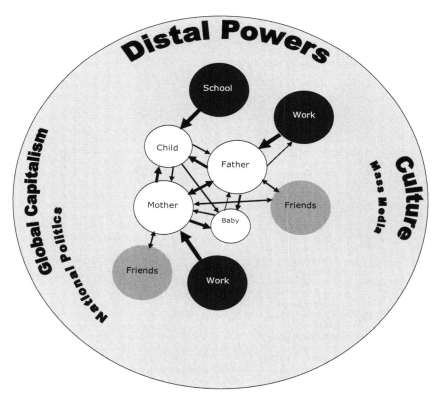

Figure 2.2 Proximal Relations

work situation affects him massively, and by extension his family, his ability to influence it is (unless he is well up the hierarchy) likely to be slight.

From the family's perspective, the father mediates a view of power that extends not much further than his workplace, but what seems to them a matter of the good will or otherwise of his managers, the cooperativeness or recalcitrance of his fellow workers, and so on, may in fact be much more a product of economic policies determined beyond even national borders.

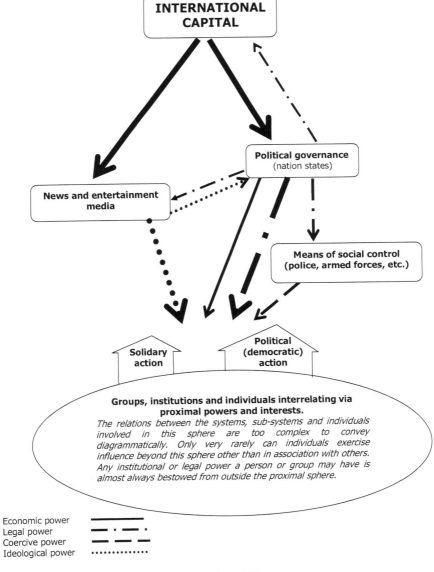

Figure 2.3 Distal Powers

Distal powers

Figure 2.3 outlines in slightly more detail some of the principal relations between the distal powers that shape our lives, often beyond our awareness. Even when an atomised consumer at the very base of the social pyramid gets some idea of the nature of the influences bearing down from afar, there is likely to be nothing much he or she can do about it except in association with large numbers of others. It seems likely that this has not been lost on national governments within recent times, and the break-up of society into 'individuals and their families', the systematic weakening of trade unions, and so on, reflects pressures of neo-liberal capitalism for which governments themselves are merely conduits.

For the most part, however, the average person is likely to have very little idea of how distal influences affect daily life, or indeed that there are such influences. Psychology will be absolutely no help in correcting such ignorance. Far from helping people understand how their conduct is constrained by the action of powers well beyond their ken, psychology focuses them instead on an 'inner world' of ideality that doesn't even escape the confines of their own skulls. In this, I suspect, psychologists have been misled by much the same factors as those that make the ordinary person's experience seem indubitable: the subjective 'evidence' for the importance of the self-as-centre is so compelling that we seem to have to look no further for the explanation of human behaviour. Further, even where the psychologist is willing to concede that distal powers probably do have some influence on individuals, the mode of such influence is likely to be seen as so vague and diffuse that it is thought irrelevant to an understanding of 'psychopathology'.

If the aim of magical voluntarist psychology is to achieve the kind of 'insight' that allows the person to see the error of their ways and adjust their conduct accordingly, the aim of a social environmentalist psychology is more or less completely the opposite: to help the person achieve 'outsight', such that the causes of distress can be demystified and the extent of their own responsibility for their condition put into its proper perspective.

Figure 2.4. suggests how the self-as-centre, in trying to understand the causes of its own conduct, is misled by the compelling brightness of its own experience. We stand, so to speak, surrounded by a horizon of power beyond which all sorts of things might be happening, but it's too dark for us to see, and in any case, apparently better than seeing, we can actually *feel* our actions as we perform them bodily. We cannot but conclude—so powerful is the impression—that the embodied sensation of action is actually its cause. However constrained—even determined—our own conduct may be, it is extremely difficult to feel it as anything other than of our own creation. This makes it very difficult for us to attribute the causes of our own conduct to their

Figure 2.4 Power Horizon

proper sources out in social space-time, and, incidentally, renders us very easy prey to pomposity, conceit and hubris. It also—more importantly from the psychologist's point of view—quickly brings to bear upon us the self-conscious spotlights of guilt and anxiety. When things go well we falsely credit ourselves with virtue; when they go badly we wrongly torment ourselves with blame. But in fact, for most of us, the power horizon is very short, and what goes on beyond it carries far more explanatory weight than our (often self-serving) idealist speculations.

A number of interesting consequences follow from the notion of 'power horizon'. One is the new meaning it gives to the concept of the 'Unconscious'. Unconsciousness ceases to be a property of individuals, and becomes an external, social phenomenon. We are unconscious of what lies in the darkness beyond our power horizon—what we cannot know or have been prevented from knowing. At the most proximal level, parents may conceal aspects of the(ir) world from children, or exercise their power to forbid access to activities or information they deem unsuitable for their children, or indeed threatening to themselves. At more distal levels, we are nearly all unconscious of the origin and manner of transmission of powers which affect our lives in all kinds of crucial and intimate ways, not because of our own stupidity or wilfulness, but because they lie beyond the zone our gaze can penetrate.

A further, extremely important consequence of our limited power horizons is, of course, the opportunities which are opened up for the more or less deliberate exploitation of our perspective. The globalisation of the 'free market' is one obvious area where the ruthless malpractices of Business can be shifted beyond the horizon of those most able to object. Opposition to abuses of power in 'developed' democracies can be dealt with by media manipulation and appeasement, while the most brutal exploitation of labour, etc., is shifted to places likely neither to fall readily under the eye nor to engage the feelings of the general public. What goes on in Burma, Brazil, Indonesia or Singapore is, for example, relatively easily maintained as a matter of indifference to the vast majority of voters in Britain. (It is true, of course, that readers of the broadsheets—often now sneeringly referred to as 'high-minded'—and viewers of television's intellectual safety-valves, Channel 4 and BBC2, may be to some extent apprised of what goes on further afield. But, as one BBC political commentator elegantly put it, 'The trouble is, it's a tabloid world,' in which it matters little what goes into high minds.)

It is also worth noting how the limited reach of our personal memories through time hugely facilitates the recycling of fashion and the maintenance of obsolescence, the disruption of ongoing organised resistance (again one thinks of the demise of unionism, whose ideological origins are by now totally obscure to most people), and the ability to veil in a fog of oblivion the savage iniquities upon which much of our social structure is founded. (How those who robbed and murdered their way to property and wealth have managed since to clothe themselves in the regalia of honour, virtue and distinction, is a matter for unceasing wonder.)

Interest

I suspect that most of us think of power as the application of brute force in the ruthless pursuit of gain—and hence tend to dismiss it as an explanatory concept not worthy of serious consideration for understanding human society and the nature of individual experience within it. Some forms of coercive power do, of course, work like this, but while it may well be the case that ultimately naked compulsion is what underwrites any form of power, the path to advantage and security is most often smoothed through the exploitation of interest. Because of the operation of interest, in other words, the influence of the more powerful is received by the less without any sign of the kind of pain we associate with force.

I have already noted that the concept of interest features hardly at all in psychology, and—more surprisingly—very little in sociological texts either. It is true, of course, that Jürgen Habermas contributed his classic *Knowledge and Human Interests* in 1968, in which he elaborated the technical, practical and emancipatory interests that underlie knowledge, and well before him Max Weber noted in *The Protestant Ethic and the Spirit of Capitalism* that '[M]en's commercial and social interests do tend to determine their opinions and attitudes.'[2] But even though modern writers may refer to 'interest' in the informal, conversational way that any of us might, it does not seem to have taken root as an explanatory concept of real theoretical importance.

This may in part be because the notion of 'interest' is already implicit in the much more familiar concepts of 'need' and 'drive'. Interests, I suggest, are, like drives and needs, determined by our nature as embodied beings, and stem from such biological necessities as food, sex, security, pain avoidance and pleasure, and shade into the rather more obviously social requirements for attachment, association, money and status. But interests, seen in this sense, are not *additional to* needs and drives so much as *replacements of* them. The crucial theoretical point I'm trying to make is that by conceiving of 'drives' as 'interests' we turn traditional psychology *inside out*, so that rather than seeing individuals as *pushed from within* by various urges and desires for which, ultimately, they are personally responsible, they are *pulled from without* by the social manipulation of, in the last analysis, inescapable biological features of being human. Sensible explanations of conduct are, then, more to be found in the complex structure of the social environment than they are in the *relatively* simple features of embodiment that we all share. I am arguing, therefore, not for an entirely new psychological concept called 'interest', but for a *change in perspective* that conceives of 'motivation' not as individual and internal, but as social and environmental.

In this way, what will almost always be needed if we are to understand people's conduct, as well as their subjective experience, is an analysis of the network of relations of power and interest in which they find themselves. It is not so much people's intentions, decisions, beliefs and wishes that count, but the ways in which they, via their interests, are and have been caught up in the swirling currents of power in the world around them.

Interests could be said to be *satisfied, frustrated, imposed or mystified* by powers. That is to say, people's conduct may be influenced through fulfilling desires ('positive reinforcement' in behaviourist terms), or blocking (or threatening to block) aspirations. Power may be applied more ruthlessly to impose offers that can't be refused or to manipulate the perceptions people have of their interests.

Powers may be *received* (by interests) or *resisted* (by counter-powers). Reception affords by far the most efficient transmission of power. It is, for example, a particular strategy of modern consumer capitalism to reduce as far as possible inhibitions standing in the way of the self-indulgence and greed upon which an ever-expanding market depends—what might be called the deregulation of pleasure.

Interests cannot be satisfied without power, nor can powers be resisted without counter-power.

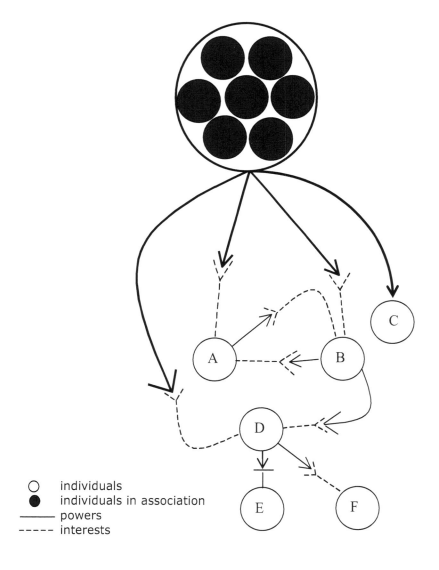

Figure 2.5 Power/Interest Interaction

Powers may be applied to *satisfy* their own interests (e.g. for security and/or advantage) or the interests of others (protection, love, altruism).

It is already obvious that a complete account of why any given individual acts as s/he does at any one time would be enormously complex, involving the interactions of power and interest not just between individuals, but between systems and sub-systems within proximal and distal social space-time. The best analogy I can think of to characterise this situation is to conceive of individuals rather as neurons in the central nervous system, where the 'electrical impulse' of conduction is replaced by *power* and the 'neurotransmitter' by *interest*—to try fully to understand an individual action in these circumstances would be like trying to spell out all the antecedents of the firing of an individual nerve cell.

Figure 2.5 (above) gives a highly simplified impression of the power/interest interactions between a proximal system (say, an employer) and some of the individuals affected by it. Most power in the diagram is transmitted through receptive interests and (as it happens) is *transitive*, that is flows through a given individual and on to others (though possibly in a modified form—e.g. an increase in pay or a change in shift-working may result in improved family relations). In the case of individual F the flow of power does not pass on to anyone else, and so is *intransitive*. Power is resisted by E through the application of counter-power, but the unfortunate C succumbs to the brute imposition of (in this case intransitive) power.

Even though trying to give anything like an adequate account of why a given person acts as they do in a given situation would require an analysis of dizzying complexity, it may nevertheless improve our 'clinical' understanding to acknowledge power/interest interactions are crucial to any such account. Complexity—even, ultimately, complexity that is in practice impossible to unravel—cannot be a reason for ignoring the importance of social systems and sub-systems to individual conduct.

The most important feature of this kind of social-materialist account for the understanding of distress is to shift the perspective from which the individual is viewed from inside to outside, from interior ideality to exterior environment. Figure 2.6 (arising from work with community psychologist colleagues in Nottingham and in collaboration with Teresa Hagan in Sheffield)[3] suggests how a person's 'psychological' difficulties may be cast in terms not of personal dysfunction (as is usually the case), but rather of environmental assets and liabilities.

It is important to emphasise that there is nothing sacrosanct about the individual segments that go to make up the principal quadrants of Figure 2.6. The intention here is to *exemplify* the way the main proximal fields of a person's social context (home life, family life, etc.) may be divided into a range of sub-

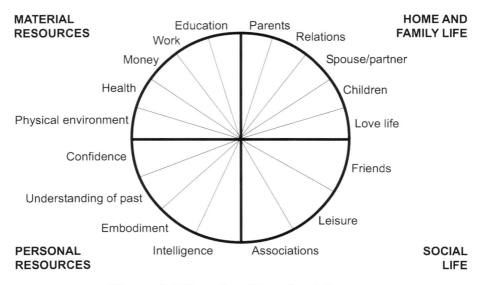

Figure 2.6 Terrain of Proximal Powers

areas that can be considered more or less discretely as positive or negative influences. These may vary from person to person and can only ever be identified through collaboration with them. A spouse or partner, for example, may for a particular individual be a source of positive support or a baleful, undermining presence—or indeed, over time, both. For many people an enquiry into their financial circumstances is likely to be a good deal more revealing as a source of psychological distress than is placing their sex lives under a Freudian microscope.

The quadrant 'personal resources' is intended to represent proximal powers that have been acquired, and embodied, over time. Attributes identified here are to be understood not as individual psychological traits, but as powers having their origin in the social world (e.g. self-confidence—see below) or biological attributes heavily valued by the social world (e.g. physical attractiveness), or mixtures of both (e.g. intelligence).

By the use of this kind of approach, a person might be encouraged to recognise that aspects of their lives they had seen as personal faults or inadequacies may more accurately be understood as deficits within their social environment, and possibly that where such deficits can be identified it may be within their power to correct them to some extent—for example a socially isolated person might be able to seek new friendship groups, and so on.

While 'power-mapping' of this kind may form a principal strand of enquiry in 'clinical' work,[4] one needs to be cautious about thinking of it as a 'therapeutic tool'. Lack of power—certainly a major source of emotional distress—is a material circumstance, not a psychological condition. The temptation for psychologists whose stock in trade is the practice of 'cognitive-behavioural therapy' is to convert powerlessness into a 'sense of disempowerment' that can be 'treated' by persuading people to see things in a different light. The point of the kind of approach advocated here is precisely to avoid that kind of error: people may or may not be able through their own efforts to compensate for deficits in their social environments or to bring counter-power to bear on noxious influences, and the object of the exercise is absolutely not to make them (feel) responsible for circumstances well beyond their control.

It is, indeed, often enough the case that people can do little or nothing about their lot. Even though this undoubtedly does throw into relief the limits of psychotherapy and counselling, it is not a matter for therapeutic despair: it is a much greater psychological gain for people to be relieved of the responsibility for things they cannot help than it is for them to be burdened a) with 'responsibility' for their state and b) with their inability to put it right.

Language

It is not possible to gain a critical understanding of the sphere of ideality in which psychotherapy and counselling establish their roots without considering in some detail the role of language. Therapy is indeed the 'talking cure' par excellence, and it is not just what therapist and client say to each other that is significant, but also what the protagonists say to themselves. But if the enterprise is to have any validity—if, that is to say, it is to *mean* anything—this world of words with which we are all so familiar must have some reference beyond itself. In the course of considering this issue we shall take a particularly searching look at some of the verbal constructions most crucial to therapeutic psychology, such as 'motives', 'insight', 'cognition' and 'self'.

Our propensity for reflecting about ourselves, for weighing and assessing the evidence of our senses, for comparing, anticipating and judging, all depend on our learning to use words. The use of language permits us to extend our society, materially and conceptually, illimitably further than any other group of animals could conceivably achieve, and indeed it is essentially our linguistic ability which defines our intelligence. In our everyday sense of ourselves, however, we consistently overlook the extent to which what we take to be individual, interior aspects of our personal 'psychology' are in fact extremely fallible social constructions, culturally acquired via language.

For what we take to be *causal* process of thought, decision and will are frequently little more than a kind of commentary that accompanies our actions. As we grow up we learn to attach words to our activities that, if we're not almost superhumanly attentive, come in our understanding to replace the activities themselves. An awareness that we are pushed and pulled by, quite literally, the force of circumstances gives way (if indeed it was ever perceptibly developed) to a conviction that our commentary on these events actually gives rise to them. As Lev Vigotsky argued so powerfully,[5] the child's thought is not somehow simply internally generated, but is acquired from the social context. Thinking is self-talk which has become silent.

Many of the characteristics that we tend to regard as entirely 'psychological' are acquired from outside. The most significant case in point is probably 'self-confidence', the crumbling of which is so often at the root of the kind of personal distress which can be 'diagnosed' by the experts as 'neurotic'.

Confidence in themselves is acquired by children as they grow up through the confidence powerful others place in them. Just as children learn to think by hearing what others say to and about them, so they learn to assess themselves according to how they are actually treated. What feels like an entirely internal faculty, a kind of moral property which ought to be under the individual's personal control, is characteristic that has become embodied over time and can no more be changed at will than can the language we speak.

'Motives'

In psychotherapy and counselling, as much as or perhaps even more than in everyday life, we take it as of the first importance to establish what we see as the *interior validity* of people's utterances, acts and intentions. We feel a strong need, that is, to establish the purity or otherwise of the 'motives' supposedly underlying their words.

In therapy, for example, the concept of 'insight' is crucial: in order to be able to act in accordance with therapeutic prescription, it is felt, the individual must be able to *see into* the internal processes which cause resistance or compliance, for it is these which provide the motivation for his or her overt conduct. Again, some humanistic psychologies, borrowing from existentialism, lay great emphasis on 'authenticity' as a prerequisite for morally sound and 'healthy' conduct: there needs to be, that is to say, a kind of harmony between inner intentions and the outer expression of them.

In everyday social life the transparency and sincerity of what others say and do is considered an important factor in establishing their trustworthiness—politicians, for example, are likely to be judged more on their perceived 'sincerity' than on the policies they advocate and institute.

In these instances we are again, I believe, confusing *commentary* with the existence of an interior 'psychological' world which, we feel, needs to be accessed therapeutically and inspected morally if we are to remain healthy, adjusted and properly disciplined citizens.

In reality, however, there is no such interior world, and in my view the concepts which are thought to arise from it can be better accounted for by considering the relations between, on the one hand, what we tell ourselves (i.e. what I have called 'commentary'), and, on the other, what we do, what we feel, what we tell others, and what can be established objectively. The table below attempts to clarify this view.

		accords with:-			
	my actions	what I feel	my account to others	the best available account	RESULT
				YES	Insight
		YES	YES		Sincerity
My commentary	YES	YES			Authenticity
	YES		NO		Deception
	NO	NO			Self-deception

Table 2.4 Commentary

If, therefore, my commentary—what I tell myself—accords with what can be objectively established (what I have called the 'best available account'), I can be said to have insight. If my commentary accords with what I feel and with what I tell others, I can be said to be sincere. And so on.

I do not want to claim that this schema is absolutely accurate or logically watertight—it is intended more as a model—but it does help do away with the necessity for postulating complex and ultimately mysterious internal moral and psychological entities.[6] Perhaps the most important effect of this is to shift our judgement of the validity or otherwise of what people say and do from unanalysable, supposedly interior moral impulses to an essentially exterior, social world of language and action. A world which is through and through permeable to the operations of power and understandable only in relation to them.

'Cognitions'

Much of what we take to be 'cognitive processes' consists in one form or another of commentary, or self-talk. Cognitive psychologists—especially the less sophisticated ones—often write as if decision-making processes, attitudes, beliefs and so on are independent, essentially rational 'schemata' existing somehow as causal agents in people's brains, and that they can in principle be isolated and accessed (by, say, a 'cognitive therapist') and, where necessary, altered to give more satisfactory behavioural outcomes. Much of the procedure of identifying and altering such 'cognitions' takes place through the medium of language. In this way it is felt that, at least in principle, an individual can tell you, for instance, what his or her 'attitudes' are (or at least that they can be inferred from his or her account), and that they can be altered through rational discussion. The most vociferous—and simple-minded—proponent of this kind of approach in the therapeutic world in recent times has been Albert Ellis, whose brain-child, 'Rational-Emotive Therapy', is widely practised.[7]

However, rather than being behaviour-causing schemata, localisable inside people's heads and describable by them, 'cognitions' of this kind can better be understood as social constructions, distributed throughout a network which extends far beyond the individual who appears to host them. What we so often take to be an 'attitude', for example, is little more than the commentary individuals give to account to themselves (and others) for the way they conduct themselves in a particular circumstance. People do, of course, behave *characteristically*, but they do so for reasons which are far more complex than simple cognitivism allows.

People may or may not be aware of the ways in which their interests are 'hooked' by powerful influences in social space-time, but in almost all circumstances they will be ready to offer an account of what they are doing and why, and indeed to maintain a commentary to themselves on the significance of their actions. The accuracy of any such commentary—whether delivered by individuals themselves or by independent observers—will depend upon the extent to which the social causation of the behaviour in question is transparent, and, given the limitations of their 'power horizons' (see above), it will very often not be.

The illusion that the individual is the sole originator of his or her conduct is of course nowhere more compelling than to the individual him- or herself, and it is as much as anything the conviction with which people are ready to account (through commentary) for their conduct which gives rise to the whole notion of 'cognitions'. For the most part, though, all I am aware of when I perform some action or other is the bodily processes which take place in me as I do so. I will probably have long forgotten that the names I give to these processes ('I wanted to', 'I thought that', 'I intended to', 'I meant to', 'I decided to', etc., etc.), rather than describing some self-evident, causal, internal rationality, were acquired originally from the often tentative and puzzled efforts of others trying to read the significance of my infantile adjustments to a world getting to grips with me.

Commentary consists largely of a series of guesses about the meaning of my actions based for the most part on very scant evidence, but, because of the extremely limited perspective from the self-as-centre, it *seems* to the individual involved a fairly comprehensive account of his or her (embodied) experience.

The notion of 'will' is susceptible to very much the same kind of analysis.

'Will-power'

In saying that there is *no such thing* as 'will-power', I am not suggesting that as individuals we are likely to find ourselves reluctantly compelled to act against our wishes by some inexorable alien force, and certainly not by a force of this kind which could in principle be understood and manipulated by some superior breed of scientific social engineers. This is the (*Brave New World*, *Clockwork Orange*) nightmare of those who take seriously the preposterous ambitions of scientistic psychologies such as behaviourism. Neither am I saying that the non-existence of will-power furnishes us with a kind of permanent excuse for immoral or illegal conduct.

In essence I am making quite a limited and modest claim: that there is *no internal, moral faculty innately resident inside human beings which can be called upon at times of crisis to deliver them from difficult or unwanted situations.*

This is not the same as saying that there is no such thing as 'will', or that we cannot speak legitimately of 'free will'. Will is the availability of power to an individual to direct socially acquired influence back into the environment. How 'free' the will is depends upon the *extent* of powers available to the individual in social space-time.

For everyday purposes, of course, there can be no sensible objection to people talking about 'will-power'. It's a useful, uncomplicated way of referring to the extent to which people can reasonably be expected to exercise the powers that are normally available to them. If I get fined for parking on the yellow lines I can scarcely invoke the non-existence of will-power as a defence, because the option of not parking on the yellow lines would (almost certainly) have been available to me.

The quite limited claim I am making is that when there is no power available to the individual from the social environment (either now or historically), *there is no further, or ultimate source of power upon which he or she can be expected to call simply by virtue of being human.* Disputes about 'will-power' and whether or not someone should have applied it then become questions of whether or not he or she *had access to* the necessary powers to act in the particular circumstances.

Here again the view from the self-as-centre is very misleading. It is almost impossible when one does something with difficulty or an unusual amount of effort not to credit oneself with special, *internal* powers. Our view of ourselves is not as a locus in social space *through* which power flows, but as an *agent* within which power *originates*. For when we act, all we are immediately aware of is the feelings that accompany the action, and if they are stressful, or if we find ourselves acting against the normal run of our inclinations in pursuit of some 'higher' goal, it is entirely natural that we attribute to ourselves some special power which seems to have an unusual moral cachet. In these circumstances, what we tend to do is sum up a highly complex social process in a simplified commentary which we quickly and mistakenly take to have a substantive reality of its own.

Let me emphasise that I am not intending to banish morality to the realm of the 'unscientific' or diminish the freedom and dignity of humankind. What I am suggesting is that many of the phenomena we take to be indicative of *individual* autonomy and virtue are in fact analysable only in terms of *social* factors.

The illusion of an autonomous self

Psychological attributes which are conventionally taken to be aspects of our individuality—'cognitions', 'will', etc.—are, then, principally illusions created by what I have called 'commentary'. The processes which these words attempt to describe are in fact more accurately to be seen as being distributed within the social space-time in which the individual is embedded.

This view is one which may try the patience of even the best-disposed reader, since it appears to undermine some of our most cherished notions about the human spirit. For example, I remember one well-known and highly respected (by me as by others) psychologist reacting with dismay at my suggestion that, of themselves, *ideas* cannot have power. Social solidarity, the taking up of ideas and putting them into action, may well be powerful, but an *idea* on its own can 'do' nothing.

Again, I think, we are misled in cases like this by a kind of shorthand way of thinking into a conviction that metaphors we invent (e.g., a 'powerful idea') describe real entities. In everyday conversation it is perfectly reasonable to describe an idea to which, say, millions have come to subscribe as 'powerful'. But when analytical accuracy becomes important, we need to be able to see that it is the fact that millions *have* taken it up that *makes* it powerful. If we fail to recognise this, we give up too much power to the public relations industry and the doctors of spin.

Power is a social acquisition, not an individual property. The isolated individual, uprooted from the social context, not only has no significant powers, but would be unrecognisable as a human being. The autonomy with which we credit ourselves is an illusion entirely dependent on the unreflective commentary which we generate from the self-as-centre, and which is reinforced by a host of interests to whose advantage it works.

The illusoriness of autonomy becomes apparent in everyday waking life mainly when the customary relation between conduct and commentary breaks down, and, as I have already indicated, nowhere is such breakdown more apparent than in the course of psychotherapy. Absolutely central to the experience of psychological distress for most sufferers is the awareness that their conduct bears painfully little relationship to their idea of themselves, their wishes and their striving. Their 'cognition' and their 'will', in other words, seem incapable of affecting what they do or how they feel.

At a more mundane level, it takes only a little reflection to realise that a great deal of what we tell ourselves—and, indeed, of what others tell us—is 'just talk'. All too often patently good advice, admonishments for healthier, more 'adjusted' living, etc., whether conveyed by family, friends, government departments or media gurus, fails in its purpose not because of the obstinacy or ill will of recipients, but because of the unavailability to them of the *means* to change. New Year resolutions are all very well, but along with seeing the *need* to change, we need the *power* to change.

It's true, of course, that the notion of the Unconscious was elaborated precisely to account for the contrasts between people's conscious accounts of their actions (their commentaries) and the actions themselves. However, all 'the Unconscious' does is shuffle the problems from one 'part' of the individual to another: the whole apparatus of commentary gets shoved wholesale and unmodified into an imaginary interior space even less intelligible than the one it started out in. This manoeuvre serves only to make matters more mysterious. Not only is the individual's own commentary disqualified (perhaps rightly, perhaps not), but it is replaced by the commentary of the therapist who claims to be able to discern the 'unconscious' origins of conduct buried deep within.

Apart from this gambit, psychotherapy and counselling have done almost nothing to get to grips with the disarticulation of commentary and conduct. Experimental psychologists and neuroscientists, on the other hand, have done very much better with investigating the illusoriness of 'will-power', 'decision making', and so on. Ingenious experiments strongly suggest, for example, that our actions are frequently under way *before* our awareness of having 'made a decision', and that the reasons we give for what we do are frequently confabulated after the event.[8]   Clinical neurology offers many examples of conditions in which words become catastrophically split from actions, such that patients' utterances and beliefs about what they're doing may be entirely at odds with conduct which is nevertheless in itself far from chaotic, and directed towards perfectly coherent and (to others) comprehensible ends. For example, in his book *Descartes' Error* Antonio Damasio[9] uses evidence from the observation of brain-damaged patients to suggest that mind is the product of an organism, not just a brain, and organisms are located in and mediate environments. Brain, body and environment flow into and out of each other, and what we do is by no means simply the result of the deliberations of a rational conductor sitting somewhere inside us. Michael Gazzaniga infers from split-brain research what he calls an 'interpreter' in the left cerebral hemisphere:

... whose job is to interpret our behaviour and our responses, whether cognitive or emotional, to environmental challenges. The interpreter constantly establishes a running narrative of our actions, emotions, thoughts and dreams. It is the glue that unifies our story and creates our sense of being a whole, rational agent. It brings to our bag of individual instincts the illusion that we are something other than what we are. It builds our theories about our own life, and these narratives of our past behaviour pervade our awareness.[10]

There are also clear enough intimations in ordinary experiences familiar to all of us of the disjunction between commentary and experience. The foremost of these is in dreaming. The 'commentator' (Gazzaniga's 'interpreter') is often absent in dreams themselves, and the sense commentary allows us in waking life of being somehow in charge, gives way to a mysterious world in which we are constantly surprised not only by the events which overtake us but also by our response to those events. It is often not clear which of the multiple characters in dreams is 'self' or 'other', and the identity—the feelings, intentions, even the sex—of the dreamer becomes extraordinarily fluid. The dreamer spectates rather than directs, reacts rather than commentates. What we dream is, after all, nothing but our 'own' ideas and images, and yet we are constantly surprised—sometimes even terrified—by them. In dreaming sleep the illusion of 'ownership' dies with the silencing of the commentator, and dreamers are left to observe more or less passively the ways the world flows through them.

What people who suffer psychological distress tend to become aware of is that no matter how much they want to change, no matter how hard they try, no matter what mental gymnastics they put themselves through, their experience of life stays much the same. This is so because there is no such thing as an autonomous individual. What powers we have are acquired from and distributed within our social context, some of them (the most powerful) at unreachable distances from us. The very *meaning* of our actions is not something that we can autonomously determine, but is made intelligible (or otherwise) by orders of culture (proximal as well as distal) over which we have virtually no control.

A person's character is not something he or she can choose, or indeed alter at whim, since character is held in place historically and contextually by powers and influences which are almost entirely independent of personal influence.

However outrageous some may find this 'deconstruction' of personal autonomy, I take for my evidence the experience of those who have had to struggle with suffering. I suggest, furthermore, that sooner or later it is the experience of us all.

As long as our actions accord more or less satisfactorily with our wishes and our intentions—as long, that is to say, as commentary and conduct are articulated reasonably comfortably—we are likely to subscribe happily enough to the notion of personal autonomy. When, however, as happens not infrequently in most of our lives, we find what we are doing running counter to what we want, what we thought we believed, and possibly even our best efforts, we begin to catch a glimpse of how human conduct really comes about. Our mistake at such times is to attribute our difficulties to some kind of aberration such as 'mental disorder'. We invoke 'circumstances beyond our control' only when we want to dissociate ourselves from the results of our actions; the point, rather, is that circumstances are *always* beyond our control, but most of the time not felt (or said by us) to be so.

It is not that 'selves' cannot or do not change; it is simply that significant change comes about as the result of shifts in the pattern of environmental influence, not because of the individual's personal wishes or efforts. The extent to which you can alter your 'self' will depend upon the powers available to you to alter your world. 'Therapy' may help someone to redeploy more effectively than before what powers and resources are available to him or her (which explains the oft-cited research finding that young, attractive, verbal, intelligent and successful people gain most from psychotherapy). Therapy may also provide the person with much-needed support and solidarity at times of great trouble. Beyond these entirely 'ordinary' (in Peter Lomas's sense)[11] services, however, there is no magic about therapy, and no reason to justify its becoming a professionalised form of 'treatment'.

Basic principles

In my book *The Origins of Unhappiness,*[12] published originally in 1993, I set out twenty-four statements summarising the environmentalist approach elaborated there (and extended in the current work). I did this with a certain amount of trepidation, as I felt that stating the case so baldly would reveal flaws obvious to everyone except me. However, in the decade that has passed since (during much of which these statements have also been set out in my website)[13] I have encountered virtually none of the critical reaction that I thought might be coming my way. Though there might of course be many reasons for this, I am now hopeful that there may indeed be a degree of fundamentality about these statements that makes them, if not exactly difficult to challenge, at least worthy of getting to grips with intellectually. For this reason, and also because they focus much of the argument of this chapter, I think it may be helpful to reproduce them here, though (except in the case of statement 18) without the commentary originally provided. I have made only very slight modifications:

1. A person is the interaction of a body with a world (environment).

2. By 'environment' is meant, most importantly, social space-time.

3. The environment is structured by material power.

4. Power may be coercive, economic or ideological. These may be, but are not necessarily, positively correlated.

5. Ideological power is viable only to the extent that it can be rendered material through concerted action with others.

6. The person's relation to the body is mainly one of sensation.

7. The person's relation to the environment is mainly through experience (intransitive reception of power) and action (transitive exercise of power).

8. Both the experience and the exercise of power may be benign or malign.

9. Power operates at varying distances from the person, proximally and distally. It is always mediated proximally, but may well originate distally.

10a. From an objective perspective, the absolute magnitude of power is negatively related to its proximity to the person.
10b. From a subjective perspective, the relative magnitude of power is positively related to its proximity to the person.

11. Each person operates within: a) a 'power horizon', and b) a 'memory span' which limits his/her ability to identify the reasons for proximal events and actions, including his/her own.

12. Environmental influence becomes embodied (i.e., becomes a collection of biological assets and liabilities).

13. There are no such things as 'inner worlds', but personal powers acquired (embodied) over time.

14. The extent to which a person can influence present circumstances will depend on the availability to him/her of material powers and resources, including embodied personal assets.

15. Powers and resources may be economic, cultural, educational, ideological, physical.

16. The degree to which the effects of the past can be influenced will depend on the nature and extent of their embodiment, as well as on the person's access to resources.

17. A person's 'psychology' consists of the meaning systems through and with which his/her embodied experience of the environment is understood, interpreted and represented.

18. Such meaning systems may be, for example, idiosyncratic or cultural, implicit or explicit. Even such simple distinctions as these, which may be represented on two orthogonal axes as shown, can give a theoretical coherence to psychological phenomena which, if treated as entities in 'internal space,' tend simply to multiply perplexingly without any real explanation. The schema here owes a great deal to the work of Rom Harré.[14]

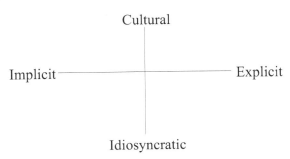

According to this schema, the character of a psychological phenomenon will be determined by its location relative to the two axes of meaning. For example a scientific production, and indeed language itself, would be found in the upper right quadrant, while some artistic productions (making explicit an idiosyncratic view) would be in the lower right quadrant; dreaming, and some forms of psychotic ideation, would be located mainly in the lower left quadrant. 'Symptoms' of distress which are commonly experienced but which people are at a loss to understand might find their place in the upper left quadrant. An example of one of these latter might be 'anorexia' (the meaning of self-starvation is almost certainly culturally determined, but remains mysteriously inarticulate; inasmuch as it becomes articulated as a demonstration—hunger strike, mortification of the flesh—it moves along to the right of the horizontal axis).

By means such as these, the curious mixed metaphors of 'dynamic' psychology—for example, the hydraulics of 'internal' space in which 'mental contents' are pushed into and out of consciousness—may be replaced by *conceptual* distinctions. Since these give coherence to phenomena which, being purely psychological, are themselves conceptual (i.e., aspects of meaning-systems), they are to be seen as operating at a meta-level.

It is important to note that psychological phenomena are not necessarily unique or private to the individual in whom they occur (i.e., who provides a locus for them), but may be aspects of cultural 'forms' established independently of specific individuals. Another way of putting this is to point out that part of the structure of personhood is beyond the skin of the individual, located not in private but in public space. Part of 'me' are the cultural factors which give shape to me. Accordingly, if cultural forms disintegrate (as with, say, conventional ideas of male and female roles) the individual is likely to *experience* this as *personal* disintegration.

19. Psychological operations may effect change only to the extent that they directly mediate, or facilitate access to, powers and resources.

20. The concept of 'will' derives from the *experience* of transmitting power, provided such transmission is congruent with the individual's wishes.

21. Freedom is proportional to the amount of power possessed by or available to the individual.

22. A person's well-being (freedom from distress) is largely determined by current circumstances and the nature and significance of his/her embodied experience and exercise of power.

23 Clinical consultation ('therapy') operates only transiently within the person's proximal field and is therefore necessarily limited in its power to effect change.

24. Consultation consists of three main elements:
(i) provision of comfort
(ii) clarification
(iii) encouragement in the use of available powers and resources.

Notes

1. For those not familiar with it the best introduction to Pierre Bourdieu's work is probably still his classic *Distinction*, published in English by Routledge, 1986.

2. Max Weber, 1985. *The Protestant Ethic and the Spirit of Capitalism*. Unwin Paperbacks, p. 72.

3. Hagan, T. and Smail, D. 1997. Power-mapping I. Background and basic methodology. *Journal of Community and Applied Social Psychology*, 7, 257–67.

4. Hagan, T. and Smail, D. 1997. Power-mapping II. Practical application: the example of child sexual abuse. *Journal of Community and Applied Social Psychology*, 7, 269–84.

5. Lev Vigotsky, 1962. *Thought and Language*. MIT Press.

6. This account no doubt owes a lot to Gilbert Ryle's classic study *The Concept of Mind*. Hutchinson, 1949.

7. See for example A. Ellis and J.M. Whitely (eds), 1979. *Theoretical and Empirical Foundations of Rational-Emotive Therapy*. Brooks/Cole.

8. Much of the more recent of this work is usefully and accessibly summarised by Susan Blackmore (2001), Consciousness, *The Psychologist*, 14, 522–5. For a penetrating analysis of some of the most important issues see also John Cromby, 2004. Between constructionism and neuroscience. The societal co-constitution of embodied subjectivity. *Theory & Psychology, 14* (6), 797–821.

9. Antonio Damasio, *Descartes' Error*, Papermac, 1996. See also his *The Feeling of What Happens*. Vintage, 2000.

10. Gazzaniga, M.S. 1998. *The Mind's Past*. University of California Press, p.174.

11. See for example Peter Lomas, 1999. *Doing Good? Psychotherapy out of its Depth*. Oxford University Press.

12. The most recent edition of this book forms half of the double volume *The Nature of Unhappiness*. Robinson, 2001.

13. www.davidsmail.freeuk.com/axioms.htm

14. Harré, R. 1983. *Personal Being*. Blackwell.

3

The Cultural Context of Therapy

In order to make sense of the phenomena encountered in the face-to-face relations of those suffering emotional distress and those trying to help them, we need to look not inward, but outward. What therapists and counsellors and their clients do, feel and say is inevitably shaped by the web of powers and interests in which we are caught, and these have their origin in distal regions where our gaze has too often failed to penetrate.

Power, though historically omnipresent, is mercurial; if its structures were stable it would become too predictable and hence too easily undermined. What can be said about the role of therapeutic ideology in the maintenance of dominating power here and now cannot remotely be thought of as standing for all time, either past or future. Indeed, successfully to maintain its advantage, power needs to catch us off balance, to stay one step ahead. And it almost certainly will.

The capitalist counter-revolution of the late twentieth century in the West co-opted therapy as part of a technology of profit, and it did so so swiftly—in part by engaging the interests of therapists and counsellors themselves—that many, perhaps most, practitioners still find it hard to accept their complicity in a political and economic system they in all likelihood deplore (neo-conservative therapists certainly exist, but they are thin on the ground). This chapter is intended to illuminate some aspects of the context of this unwilling complicity.

The technology of profit

Apart from the latent violence that constitutes the ultimate sanction of every society (and is making an ominous reappearance at the present time), the dominating power in the modern Western world is that of money. If the last four or five hundred years are anything to go by, it seems to be a fact of political economy that money accumulates in fewer and fewer hands. With only rare bumps and hiccups to hold up its 'progress' here and there (as for example in the welfare democracies following the Second World War), society has become increasingly unequal, and at the present time the profit motive seems not only unprecedentedly rampant, but to hold sway virtually unchallenged.

Such spectacular greed, such indifference to the poverty and suffering it inflicts between and within populations across the globe, cannot be established and maintained without a technology of social control. My concern is of course with the psychological aspects of this technology and my purpose here is to elaborate on some of the factors already identified in earlier pages as contributing to the mystification of our understanding of the way the social environment works.

The maintenance of economic power in the hands of a tiny minority of the world's population is helped by the ability of the powerful to exploit our situation as isolated individuals locked within proximal worlds.

There *is* a 'real world' where the mechanics of power are manipulated to the profit of those who have learned—whether consciously or not—how to benefit from them. Though it touches on us often enough, and that most often painfully, the way the real world works is for the most part kept beyond the horizon of our ability to discern. Our preoccupations are with things closer to home: with our own economic survival and that of those close to us, with our status within the social groups we occupy locally, with everyday personal satisfactions and discomforts, with ambitions, dreams and wishes.

A characteristic of the real world is that the beings in it (including, of course, all of us) are embodied. They live and die; some thrive, some suffer. It does not suit the interests of unequal power that the hard realities of this world are too well understood by those—the vast majority—who profit from it least. For us there needs to be—and has been—created other forms of world, not real, where we may lead disembodied lives, detached from the possibility of laying living hands on the levers of power. It is a world of make-believe, where inside is indistinguishable from outside and where we may live more easily in our dreams than in our bodies.

Make-believe: a parallel universe of discourse

Our capacity as human beings for imagination and storytelling makes us exquisitely vulnerable to exploitation by those who understand the properties of ideological power. Our natural propensity to credit commentary above any more detached understanding makes us more than prepared to open our minds to versions of 'reality' which are laced with some kind of appeal to our tastes, preferences and interests. We are, one could say, naturally credulous.

The societal apparatus which exists for the manipulation of our credulity forms an absolutely essential part of the technology of power. In everyday parlance this is, of course, for the most part what we mean by 'the media'. But the news and entertainment media are not the only determinants of the way we see and interpret the world. Education and the related institutions of intellectual endeavour and instruction are also crucial to our understanding. None of this, of course, is lost on those in whose interest it is to channel the fruits of our labours into their pockets. In recent years the encroachment of Business into areas once thought (no doubt naively) to stand apart from commercial interest has been perfectly obvious. Universities fall over themselves to replace academic standards with business ones and corporate intrusion into schooling no longer causes much surprise or indignation (George Monbiot's exposure of the extraordinary influence of corporate power on the public sphere in Britain[1] caused barely a ripple).

This is not necessarily part of a consciously directed process. As I have tried to show in previous pages, conscious direction is in any case largely a myth. As money-power—capital—flows into fewer and fewer hands, it creates a network of interest that maintains and accelerates the process, rather as the streams which form the rivers and the rivers themselves as they flow to the sea may carve their beds more deeply. As Adam Smith is famed for noting, there is indeed a degree of impersonality in the way 'the market' structures itself which side-steps the will of those who become caught up in it.

In this way the interests of significant, if relatively small, sections of society become hitched to the necessary process of disguising the fact that a system designed to maximise the profits of a few cannot at the same time run to the advantage of the many. The growth of advertising and public relations, the arrival on the political scene of a new profession of 'spin-doctor', etc., testify to the importance of controlling public perception. Apart from those summoned to the financial elite who manage the economy of the 'free market', the best and brightest of our youth are recruited to the media of make-believe. Making people believe that what is least is in fact most in their interest has become a societal task of the first importance.

Once again, the attribution of greater reality to words than to worlds is already prefigured in the almost irresistible priority we accord as we grow up to commentary. Pretty well everybody is in this way primed to attach enormous importance to language, and I would not want to suggest that this phenomenon is in any way the invention of a cynical controlling power. It does not have to be conspiracy that rules our society (though sometimes it may be), but merely the sliding together of the interests which oil the wheels.

Over the twentieth century academic philosophy, in making the obvious point that there is no directly knowable Reality, came more and more to credit the importance of language and to deny that there is any point at all in speculating about what might lie beyond it. There is nothing, said Derrida, outside the text;

popular readings of Foucault privilege 'discourse' above all else; Rorty scoffs at the idea that our understanding could 'hold a mirror up to nature'.

While these philosophers have serious points to make, their standpoint lends itself wonderfully well to a society which seeks ideologically to detach its citizens from their embodied relation to a material world. Serious intellectuals seem to be the last to anticipate the use to which their work will be put. When, for example, Jean Baudrillard writes[2] of the 'hyperreality' created by unfettered consumerism, it is all too easy for the edge of critical irony to be lost from his text and for it to become a kind of sourcebook for marketing executives, admen and other cultural illusionists. The whole notion of 'postmodernism' becomes popularised as the cutting edge of social and intellectual progress, distracting us from the (much more comprehensible) insight that what we are involved in is in fact a recycling of high capitalist economic strategies which reached a previous peak seventy or eighty years ago.

Psychology also has played an enormous part in helping to de-materialise the Western world over the past century. Freud managed to represent the significance of our experience as not only all in the mind, but most of it in the 'unconscious mind', such that it became well and truly impossible for us to criticise our world (just to criticise our *selves*, and that only with the help of a professional psychoanalyst). As I have already noted, for much of psychology what goes on in the world, what the material relations are between individual and society, are matters of complete irrelevance. All that counts is what goes on inside the individual's head. Whatever the benefits of this view in terms of the hope it may bring to people of controlling their fate, it is an absolute godsend to those who have a less rarefied grasp of how to make the world work to their advantage. Thieves sack the mansion undisturbed while its occupants remain sunk in their dreams.

In her book *No Logo*,[3] Naomi Klein demonstrated how uninterested many modern corporations are in the actual material products that carry their brand. The products themselves may in fact be manufactured at rock-bottom cost by contractors located in 'export processing zones' in the developing world, with competing labels 'often produced side by side in the same factories, glued by the very same workers, stitched and soldered on the very same machines'. The 'value added', the vastly inflated costs of these objects which go to feed the corporate structure, is what is crucial: and it is spun out of nothing, pure marketing make-believe.

If, as I sometimes think it is, Psychology is the greatest intellectual confidence trick of the twentieth century, it is one whose sheer economic importance is not to be underestimated!

Effectively, then, we find ourselves cut loose in a world of words where what is true and real is a matter of what we can be persuaded to believe. Those who profit most from this state of affairs will be those best able a) to control the use of language and b) to exploit the capacity of language to introduce us to an infinity of 'realities'.

In *The Origins of Unhappiness* I described the way in which the conceptual frame of Business came during the 1980s to be imposed right across the cultural board. No established social practice or institution was left out: education, health, sport, leisure and travel—and of course government itself—all were flooded with the same debased and simplistic language of business and accountancy. Absolute values such as Truth and Right, features of the now discredited Enlightenment, were replaced with the crude market criteria of what pays. Nothing has changed since to impede this process.

Whoever controls language, controls thought. We now have installed at the heart of our culture a generation barely able to think outside the parameters of business. 'Reality' is described and experienced in terms of competition, cost and profit; worth is judged in terms of wealth and status. The whole conceptual and linguistic register of our lives has been collapsed into one dimension, and with it our capacity to experience ourselves as anything other than business successes or failures: what matters is not the contribution you make to the social world, but how much money you can make from it. Nowhere is this more obvious than in the once idealistic youth of our universities—it is commonplace, for example, to come across students of medicine who, seriously worried about the money and status attached to their proposed career, yearn instead to become management consultants. Not to have a Mercedes by the time you're thirty is to have failed in your life's project.

The philosophical subtlety that at the highest intellectual level acknowledges the *relativity* imparted by discourse to our ideas of reality is, however, by no means reflected in the 'tabloid world' we are now forced to inhabit. The reality which Business culture and ideology offers us is not presented as one alternative among several, but as 'the real world' to which all of us must shape up if we are not to end up hopelessly at the bottom of the heap.

Fuelling the cynicism of 'spin' is an expectation that the person-in-the-street will assume a fairly direct linkage between descriptions of the world and the world itself. What ordinary people think, what they conceive of as the truth, is of the utmost importance as their actions (particularly of course, their actions as consumers) are likely to be based upon it. The best, most convincing *description* of the way things are comes in this way actually to constitute how they are 'in fact'. The traditional struggle to *represent* the world in words is replaced by a struggle to *create* a world in words. The success or otherwise of this project is measured in terms of 'credibility'.

This is the universe of discourse where the spin-doctors dwell, but the world in which it places us is a strangely fragile one. For although the media and marketing technocrats vie with each other to foist upon us that 'reality' most profitable to themselves and to the influences which control them, it becomes pretty obvious that we are not talking here about what most people think of as reality, but about make-believe of differing degrees of credibility.

At the heart of this whole enterprise, then, there is a contradiction: 'credibility'—what people can be persuaded to believe—is the ultimate goal of 'spin', but in the popular mind their remains an indissoluble, though inarticulate, link between what is believable and what is real or true. Credible worlds, in other words, are *not* the same as real ones. Business fakes a world which it sells us as the truth, but is fatally undermined by the truth that lies beyond it.

Just occasionally the universe of discourse suffers a rude intrusion of reality which somehow catches us all out, and we are left open-mouthed, not knowing quite what to make of our situation. The story of the railway network in Britain around the turn of the twenty-first century provides an excellent example.

Despite a series of accidents, some very serious and some minor, and an unremitting history of cancellations and delays, the management of the privatised rail companies claimed to be providing a steadily improving service in which safety was their first priority. Throughout the system the experience of failure was met with evasive assurances and oddly recurring excuses (e.g. that lateness was due to a bridge having been 'struck by a motor vehicle'.) To be a passenger was like entering a virtual world in which a pretence of (thwarted) efficiency consistently blanketed the actuality of cancelled trains and late arrivals, cold waits on decaying stations and missed appointments.

Then, in October 2000, a broken rail brought an express train off the track near Hatfield, killing four people and injuring many others. Suddenly reality broke through. The safety which had before been spun as 'number one priority' now became a priority in fact. Apparently overnight, 1000 miles of track became suspect and over 200 speed restrictions were imposed. At two hours' notice the line between Glasgow and Carlisle was closed. Senior managers of Rail Track, the company mainly involved, appeared on television like penitent schoolboys caught red-handed in some embarrassing misdemeanour. In an instant, it seemed, passengers had become embodied and the railways and rolling stock rematerialised as objects in a real world.

Language need not in fact be simply the means whereby we create an infinity of relative worlds (that is to say, a snare and delusion). On the contrary, it may be used in the struggle to decode our experience of reality, to give us a sense of what is *actually* happening in the world. Precisely the point of the Business take-over of language, of the frenetic collective voice of the media, is to drown out the possibility of our articulating to ourselves the nature of the reality in which we are caught up.

The first task of any oppressive power is to strip the subjective voice, the languaged sensibility of the embodied person, of authority. If you are to be gulled by the make-believe of the public relations world, the last thing you must be permitted to credit is the evidence of your own senses (that is a matter for 'experts'). This is because the ability of the individual, embodied subject to evaluate the evidence of his or her experience is the ultimate defence against illusion.

I do not mean to imply that our subjective experience is infallible. The vulnerability of personal experience to error—i.e., of being wrongly interpreted in words—means that we need to take great care to check on its validity before we act on it in any irretrievable way (this process, in fact, constitutes the heart of scientific method). The subjective perspective needs to be evaluated *inter*subjectively (which brings it as near as possible to being objective) but there is still, ultimately, no *authority* beyond it. Furthermore, the representation to ourselves of our own experience, and the processes of checking it against the experience of others, all take place in the medium of language. The fallibility and imprecision of words give us plenty of reason for being careful with how we use them, but no reason at all for abandoning our project of trying to understand the world.

There has, over decades, been an unremitting onslaught against the art and science of interpreting one's own experience, to such an extent that many people—consciously or unconsciously—find it impossible to have an opinion without the prostheses of the media or the prescriptions of one or other of our modern doctors of meaning. The first task of any rebellion against Business dominance is to re-establish the integrity of the universe of discourse; that is to say, to return to the search for words that describe the world as accurately as possible.

In order to maximise its effectiveness, consumer capitalism, the engine of profit, needs to detach individuals from an accurate understanding of, and significant influence within, the social and material environment they occupy. The ideal unit of consumption (i.e. person), utterly vulnerable to the interests and influences of 'the market', is:

a) *dissociated*—unable to form solidarity with others, and hence

b) *disempowered*

c) *dislocated* from any reliable anchorage in the material environment from where resistance could be mounted.

d) *disembodied*—e.g., psychologically 'freed' from the limitations which embodiment places on his or her ability to consume.

Social space-time must become so blurred, so insubstantial, that the person becomes entirely dependent, materially and psychologically, on the reality which is offered him or her through the manufactories of make-believe which we recognise collectively as 'the media'. Apart from establishing control over language, and hence what I have called 'commentary' (and so thought itself), a primary aim of economic exploitation is to collapse the distinction between inside and outside.

Outside is the real world in which we are embodied and live our lives with others. Inside is the psychologically manipulable world of imagination where we can be *made to believe*, but where also, it is important to note, we host personal powers and resources which (though originating from without) can be seen as in a sense our individual 'property'. Thus, on the one hand, the potentialities of imagination may be recruited to mask the realities of our existence, while on the other those personal powers and resources which we might potentially be able to develop to our advantage and (in the broadest sense) enrichment must be extracted from us and sold back to us as commodities.

In this way, the *world* is turned outside in such that, among other things, real exploitation and deprivation are represented and experienced as essentially *psychological* failures. Correspondingly, *people* are turned inside out such that, among other things, any real (embodied) powers or abilities they may have acquired are externalised, commodified and marketed.

Outside in: Making the public private
Psychology is the principal tool which has been used to privatise the public world in which actions really count. Almost by definition, the focus of psychology is on what goes on, supposedly, inside the isolated individual. The private world of beliefs, desires, disembodied thoughts and 'cognitions' becomes the arena in which we believe we have to operate in order to change our lives. This, as I have already suggested, is indistinguishable from belief in magic, for it places us in an immaterial, interior world whose main contacts with external reality are *wishful* rather than *actual*. It is absolutely no accident that there has in recent years been a resurgence in frankly magical and religious systems of belief and that these have become increasingly interwoven (as in 'alternative medicine') with popular conceptions of science. What we fail to recognise is that, certainly in the psychological sphere, what we take to be 'scientific' *is* for the most part magic.

The prevention of individual citizens' participation in public space is the central strategy of a programme of systematic disempowerment which leaves the resources of the material world exposed unresistingly to corporate plunder. Politics is virtually eradicated—the 'third way' announces an end to conflict of interest, and in a sense this is all too true: the only interests left are those of big business, which rules largely undisturbed by the opposition of those (the vast majority) whom it damages. As I shall elaborate when I come to consider the concept of 'responsibility', the social havoc that is wreaked by unfettered economic greed comes to be interiorised as the personal weakness and irresponsibility of those principally affected.

The struggle of ordinary people to retain the commons—lost over centuries of land enclosure—has now shifted onto psychological grounds. The individual is driven out of public space in countless, almost imperceptible steps, many of which are mystified as somehow 'person-friendly'. Note, for example, the disappearing use of surnames in British culture. This is part of a process of 'impersonalisation' in which that element that gives to *anyone* a *public* role is eradicated. The telephone salesperson, the functionary who fields your enquiry or complaint has no *identity* beyond the anonymous first name that goes with the parroted 'How may I help?'—not only is there no space in which they can be located and held accountable, there is nowhere for them to *signify*, to be agents in public space. This is just about the purest obliteration of the distinction between inside and outside, for just as one is robbed of public dignity, so also the bestowal of intimacy which use of the first name gives is tipped out into a world of universal indifference. To have a surname and title is now no longer accorded as of right to all, but has become a prerogative of the relatively powerful, that is those who can lay some claim to be influential in public space. The rest of us will be known only by our first names, very much as plantation slaves used to be: not as an indication of the private affection in which we are held, but as a mark of contempt for our insignificance.

For most of us, real life is experienced as a kind of frustrating barrier to admission to the 'hyperreality' held before us by the media, the heaven-on-earth where the rich and famous, the celebrities and the lottery-rich enjoy the rewards of their virtue, their talent and their luck. Where formerly people were pacified with a prospect of paradise, the modern mass consumer is mesmerised by the outside chance of admission to the real Olympus where the modern incarnations of the old gods dwell and disport themselves, sometimes indeed crossing its fortified barriers to allow us to touch or be touched by them.

Apart from the small but undying hope that good fortune may gain us entry, the most the rest of us can hope for is to live vicariously on the controlled visits allowed us by the celebs into their world. We may, for example, stand on the outside looking in, like the crowds at the crush barriers of a film premiere, and we will be drip-fed a certain degree of manufactured intimacy with them as the beautiful people confess their secrets on the talk-shows and invoke (or fall victim to) the public relations machinery that surrounds them.

We are not readily invited to go behind the scenes of this theatre in order to observe how and by whom its world is created and populated, its players cast, their masks selected. Still less are we allowed a glimpse into the real halls of power where the big deals are struck and the big money made, nor into the haunts and homes of those who make it. For the glamorous world of celebrity is the principal vehicle of an ideology of interiority which would become rapidly called into question if the general populace got too clear a view of how things really work.

Although, of course, the ephemerality of fashion cannot be disguised, we still believe that the celebrity, the famous 'personality', somehow deserves his or her elevation by virtue of individual qualities (even if only physical beauty) which are somehow to his or her personal credit. Celebrity, in other words, is presented as personal achievement, thus making the rest of us look like—if not failures—people who have not got what it takes to make it past the boundaries of ordinary life.

However, what looks like personal 'charisma', 'star quality', etc., is on the whole the capricious gift of a publicity machine that runs on energy supplied by a far more sordid world. Though, of course, some occupants of hyperreality have been constructed on the basis of a degree of embodied talent (e.g. sporting stars), this quickly becomes inflated and exploited far beyond any reasonable assessment of its original significance or true social worth. For the most part, celebrity is the creation of a media industry built to uphold an ideology, and it is the ideology that matters, not its creatures. 'Charisma' is but the visible aspect of a power which does not originate within the individual celebrity, but is accorded him or her by the puppeteers of the media world; and it can, of course, be instantly withdrawn, the star eclipsed. (Media people know well enough their strength, as anyone who has encountered the arrogant, blasé exercise of their dominion will be able to affirm.)

I am not, of course, saying anything here which is not already well known and widely discussed. What I think we do not see so clearly, however, is the degree to which this faked world that lies beyond our actual lives really does pollute our existence. Despite its shoddiness and insubstantiality it really is a vast constituent of our environment, and inevitably flows through us such that we come to accept the premises on which it is built even if we react against some of the crudity of its expression. Not only does it serve to blunt our critical faculties, to 'dumb us down' and divert our energy inward to the satisfaction of artificially created needs; not only does it reinforce a mythology of personal worth based on the individual exercise of interior powers: but it places us within an inescapably and unremittingly painful situation where the *actuality* of our lives is constantly undermined. We are, that is to say, thrown into a state of pervasive uncertainty and insecurity over how far we are from coming up to scratch, from breaking out of the grey limbo that is our existence into the bright world the other side of the television screen.

There are other ways, too, in which we are induced to host as our personal failings the iniquities of the outside world.

In his masterly analysis of the effects of French colonial rule in North Africa, Frantz Fanon[4] demonstrated how the impress of distal power can end up as hatred and strife among the oppressed groups themselves, thus apparently legitimising conceptions of the ruled by the rulers as, for example, genetically tainted, psychologically inferior or 'mentally ill'. A similar process is in my view involved in some aspects of what has come to be known as 'political correctness', the typically Orwellian irony of which is that they are neither political nor correct.

There is of course no disputing that in modern Western society whites often oppress blacks and men often oppress women. This is bound to be the case in a social context in which people are forced to compete for scarce resources and to differentiate themselves from each other in any way which will accord them greater power, however illusory that power may be (nothing, after all, could be more pathetic than the belief that 'whiteness' confers *personal* superiority, or that men are in some way to be valued more highly than women).

However, *it is a conceptual mistake of the first magnitude to attribute the causes of such oppression to internal characteristics or traits of those involved.* So long as sex*ism* and rac*ism* are seen as personal attitudes which the individual sinner must, so to speak, identify in and root out of his or her soul, we are distracted from locating the causes of interpersonal strife in the material operation of power at more distal levels.[5] Furthermore, *solidarity* against oppressive distal power is effectively prevented from developing within the oppressed groups, who, successfully divided, are left by their rulers to squabble amongst themselves, exactly as Fanon detailed in the case of Algerians impoverished and embittered by their French colonial masters.

It is not that racist or sexist attitudes do not exist—they may indeed be features of the commentary of those who exercise or seek to exercise oppressive, possibly brutal proximal power. But that commentary is not the *cause* of the process that results in such proximal oppression, and it is as futile to tackle the problem at that level as it is to try to cure 'neurosis' by tinkering with so-called 'cognitions' or 'unconscious motivation'.

This, I think, goes some way to explaining the otherwise puzzling success of 'political correctness' at a time when corporate power extended its influence over global society on an unprecedented scale. For this success was in fact no triumph of liberal thought or ethics, but rather the 'interiorising', the turning outside in of forms of domination which are real enough. The best-intentioned among us become absorbed in a kind of interior witch-hunt in which we try to track down non-existent demons within our 'inner worlds', while in the world outside the exploitation of the poor by the rich (correlating, of course, very much with black and white respectively) and the morale-sapping strife between men and women rage unabated.

Once again, we are stuck with the immaterial processes of 'psychology', unable to think beyond those aspects of commentary we take to indicate, for example, 'attitudes' or 'intentions'. The history of the twentieth century should have taught us that anyone will be racist in the appropriate set of circumstances. What is important for our understanding is an analysis of those circumstances, not an orgy of righteous accusation and agonised soul searching.

Inside Out

What makes the 'inner world' so important to us is that it is where we experience our lives. There is, of course, no 'world' there at all, but a wonderful confusion of feeling and imagination, thinking, dreaming and memory that furnishes our personal idea of what it is to be human and to be alive. It constitutes our subjectivity.

It is, I believe, a profoundly ironic paradox that modern psychology has done more than anything else to divert us from an understanding and appreciation of the subjective experience of self. Instead of a delicate, modest, tentative, respectful consideration of the unfathomably chaotic, sometimes extraordinarily beautiful, sometimes horrifically frightening, always wildly idiosyncratic interior which is to be found within each one of us, psychology has tried to unpick us with a kind of fastidious distaste that has nothing to do with respect or love and everything to do with discipline.

At least in part because of the success of the psychological enterprise, we are as individuals largely unable to celebrate and rejoice in the experience of self; but rather, when we have to, turn our gaze inward with deep apprehension for what we may find there. What we find, certainly, is a person like no other— and that is one of the principal causes of our misery.

For psychology has imposed on our subjectivity an entirely inappropriate normativeness, a narrow set of moral and aesthetic prescriptions which turns each one of us into a kind of self-diagnosing psychiatric inquisitor, ready to infer from the recognition of each new feeling pathological deviance from an ideal we think we see embodied in everyone else.

I can think of no mainstream approach to psychological therapy which doesn't harbour at its core a humourless authoritarianism, a moralistic urge to control, that has the ultimate effect of causing infinitely more pain than it could ever conceivably hope to cure. Invested with the authority our social institutions accord it, psychology pokes its fingers into our souls and, pronouncing disapprovingly on what it thinks it reveals, spreads dismay and despondency among the populace.

For you don't have to have been near a psychologist or psychiatrist to have been infected with the cultural dread of being different. Far from having supported the individual's sense of subjectivity, psychology has assisted in throwing it into question to the point that the principal concern of many of us is to hide from others what we fear to be inside ourselves.

The privilege of having been able to talk to thousands of people over the years in a setting that minimises threat (and so the need for self-defence) makes possible a few generalisations that come just about as close to 'psychological laws' as anything one is likely to encounter. For example:

- Absolutely everybody wants to be liked.
- Everyone feels different inside (less confident, less able, etc.) from how they infer other people to feel.
- Few honest and courageous people who have achieved anything of real value in life do not feel a fraud much of the time.

Acceptance of these three 'laws' alone would save an awful lot of people a good deal of grief!

What we *think* should be inside ourselves seems to be a kind of anodyne pastiche of the model of humanity fed us by the advertising industry, or possibly the kind of cold, confident *Übermensch* of the TV fantasy hero or heroine—calculated, controlled, super-competent in money, war and sex.

In contrast to this, however, what resides within is the tangle of sensitivity and eccentricity that truly reflects our individual subjectivity. It couldn't really be otherwise: we *are* all different because we have come from different places at different times with different people. No two people have the same experience of the world. It is impossible to overestimate the importance of this diversity; instead of attempting to discipline our subjective individuality, to iron out interior differences in accordance with a regulatory ideal of 'normality', we should appreciate this inner chaos as reflecting the raw material of our *significance* as human beings.

However, the material of subjectivity is indeed raw, and its significance is lost without a public world that can structure it and give it expression. For our private experience to mean anything, for its value to be realised, it has to be accommodated within a 'commons'—within public space—that *recognises it as a contribution*. In order for this to happen, public space has to be sufficiently structured, sufficiently attuned to the enormously wide scale of human experience and the ways of human embodiment, to receive, make sense of and use constructively what each of us has to offer.

A life is given meaning and value not by being 'enjoyed' in private, but by being lived and appreciated in public. Even the most tortured private experience can find dignity as well as worth if there exists to receive it a convivial social world where human beings act with and for each other. This is not what happens when the overriding principle of social life is profit.

Rather than *validating* private experience, consumerist society *exploits* it. In this situation we are not able to use whatever we know of life to contribute to the well-functioning of the whole, but have such knowledge extracted from us and sold back to us in the form of commodities. Just about any kind of human activity, any form of spontaneous or creative action, can be analysed into its constituent parts and synthesised into a saleable object. Any even remotely identifiable human experience or feeling is dragged out of the most intimate recesses of the soul, grafted to consumer goods of one kind or another (if only in the form of an image) and offered back to us as something we could only hope to acquire commercially from outside.[6]

This is psychological privatisation—a kind of economy of spirit-laundering in which the advertising industry and the media appropriate those interior constituents of ourselves of which (not least because of a disciplinary 'psychology') we have grown deeply mistrustful, stamp upon them their commercial legitimation, and sell them back to us. We are in this way offered for our personal consumption a toxic adulteration of spiritual sustenance which had in its original form been perfectly nutritious, even if we had often been largely unaware of its role and function within us.

Consumerism exploits interiority to the point that people are almost totally drained of it. Instead of our privacy being *honoured* and our individuality being *endorsed*, our innermost feelings, hopes and fears are tipped out into the open and picked over for their commercial potential. There is no secret desire, no haunting fear, no tremulous shred of anxiety, no fragment of tenderness that will not be exposed to the jaded inspection of the market, worked over and placed on the junk stall for mass consumption.

When what was inside is relentlessly exposed to public view in this way, it is robbed of all its sustaining power, and there is left within us nothing but an emptied-out husk of impulse. Unable to draw with confidence on the wealth of our private resources—a confidence born of the *faith* that it is all right to be chaotically human—we are reduced to putting on a lifeless show of passion that has lost all personal meaning. People brought up in this culture have no endorsed experience of inside, but can only imitate the media stereotypes harnessed to consumption. Interiority becomes a simulacrum of commercially created image; a puzzle; a source of anxiety. What we are truly left with inside is those aspects of subjectivity in which the market has no interest: an inarticulate sense of futility, drudgery and loss.

One sees the results of all this particularly clearly in the psychological maladies of the young—maladies not of their *personal* being, but forms of *social* sickness arising out of the lack of fit between the subjective experience of embodied self on the one hand and the public vehicles available for giving them expression on the other.

Human bodies do not in fact change in accordance with media ideals (hence perhaps the increasing need for the creation of fantasy worlds in which to accommodate the demands of the latter). If the internal requirements and promptings of the body are to be understood, they need a public culture that recognises and gives them meanings which are both common and adequate. That is to say, we need not only to be able to refer to and enact our private experiences and impulses in ways that will be recognised and understood by others, but these public recognitions and understandings need to accommodate such experiences and impulses accurately, comfortably and productively.

People brought up in the capitalist revival of the 1980s and 90s, even though—many of them—exceptionally well provided for materially and more than adequately trained in the management of commodified relationships, often received practically no education at all in what it is to be human. Their parents, preoccupied with a scramble for security in a heartless and brutally competitive economic world, were happy enough if they could provide the requisite consumer goods and otherwise leave their children's education to 'experts'.

This generation thus depended for its understanding of itself on an unprecedentedly shallow business culture that dealt almost exclusively in commercial stereotypes and images. Emotional relationships were more likely to be formed with games consoles, computers and fantasy role-play figures than with people who were able to acknowledge, explain and interpret what goes on *inside* human beings with any degree of honesty.

Quite apart from being officially devoid of compassion and altruism, the 'Thatcherist' culture ignores any kind of human emotion or impulse that falls outside the business register. That is to say, anything *inside* that cannot be turned *outside* as a commodity, that cannot be hooked into a disciplinary economic anxiety; anything that is vague, complex, or that might bind people in solidarity rather than pitting them against each other in competition— anything like that is simply left in an incoherent, inexpressible, mysterious lump within, like a large indigestible meal that the subject cannot remember having consumed.

The result of this is to be seen as a new form of 'anxiety' in the young. The typical 'case' is a young man (men are, I suspect, marginally more vulnerable than women) who has perhaps been quite successful at school, is socially quite competent and well integrated (though friendships may be more superficial than profound), doing pretty well in his job or course of study, yet assailed periodically by anxiety that, though experienced as overwhelming, displays little outward sign of distress. What usually underlies this form of anxiety seem often to be almost banal fears, some of which are in fact the lot of all but the most fortunate human beings and some simply unavoidable emotional reactions which at other times might even have been regarded as a blessing.

For example, self-consciousness in publicly conspicuous situations, discomfort at public speaking, etc., may be experienced as something totally alien and incomprehensible, such that the individual cannot make a connection between the situation and his feelings: over and over again he may put himself into such situations in the expectation that there should be 'no problems', only to find yet again that problems there are indeed. Confusion over emotional attachments can lead to similar uncomprehending panic: falling in love seems to be something for which many young men possess no framework of understanding.

The psychologist's job at this—and, I believe, at any other—time is not to *diagnose* the 'inner person' but to *explicate* his or her relationship with the outside world. This is to switch 'professional' attention from discipline and conformity to a libertarian concern with understanding subjective distress as a function of the personal (and ultimately, of course, wider) environment.

While this may, I suppose, be viewed as a valuable form of 'therapy', there is a far more important task, and one which reaches well beyond the mere practice of psychology. This is the task which faces all of us of rebuilding a public world that *accommodates* the human subjects who go to make it up.

Notes

1. George Monbiot. *Captive State: The corporate takeover of Britain*. Macmillan, 2000.

2. Jean Baudrillard, 1981. *For a Critique of the Political Economy of the Sign*. Telos Press.

3. Naomi Klein. *No Logo*. Flamingo, 2001.

4. Frantz Fanon. *The Wretched of the Earth*. Penguin Books, 1967.

5. A persuasive statement of a very similar view is to be found in Paul Farmer, On suffering and structural violence. In A. Kleinman, V. Das and M. Lock (eds), 1997. *Social Suffering*. Univ. California Press.

6. In an excellent article in *New Internationalist,* (Eat, sleep, buy, die. *New Internationalist, 329*, November 2000) Jonathan Rowe uses almost identical words and ideas to reinforce the case:

> In economics there is no concept of enough: just a chronic yearning for more, a hunger that cannot be filled.
> This requires that all life must be converted into a commodity for sale. The result is a relentless process of enclosure. It started centuries ago with land. Today it is encroaching upon every aspect of our individual and collective beings.

Think about the growth industries today. We buy looks from plastic surgeons, mental outlooks from pharmaceutical companies, the activity of our bodies from 'health' clubs, interaction with friends from telecommunications firms, and on and on. Security comes from police departments, insurance companies and privatised prisons. Transport comes from oil and automobile companies.

Virtually every life function and process is turning into something we have to buy. And lest anyone suspect a tired ideological shtick, let's say right here that the government is a culprit too. It turns education into schooling and community into bureaucracy—much as the market turns childhood into a petri dish of nagging.

Either way, what the economists call growth becomes a process of cannibalisation. The formal economy, private and public sectors alike, takes us apart piece by piece and then sells us back to ourselves.

We must become less so that the economy can become more. Little wonder we feel drained and stressed. We become the biological counterparts of the oil wells and toxic dumps, both the raw material of the economy and the receptacles of its waste. Meanwhile, millions don't have enough to begin with.

4

Responsibility

Ever since the 'treatment of mental illness' became a serious professional enterprise, the interests of practitioners have inevitably shaped the *moral* role accorded to the individual sufferer. The problem is that these interests spawn a therapeutic ideology that is internally inconsistent, indeed contradictory.

To start with, if mental illnesses are to be considered illnesses like any other, it is necessary to represent the patient as the passive victim of biological (psychiatry) or psychological (psychotherapy) circumstances. For cure to be effected, patients must submit themselves to the appropriate professional regimen—either medical or psychological, and cannot be expected to achieve the desired outcome on their own, or indeed any other non-professional initiative.

However, it is also necessary to account for therapeutic failure. The medical-psychiatric solution to this problem is at least consistent: medical science is not perfect, more research is needed, treatments need changing or refining, drug dosages need increasing or decreasing, titrating, combining, and so forth. For the psychological approaches it is not so easy, and the solution most often preferred is an unusual one for a supposedly professional discipline, and that is to invoke the moral agency of the patient in his or her failure to 'respond to treatment'. It is here that we encounter such notions as patients' 'resistance' to the stern requirements of 'insight' that they should change their ways. Or perhaps their 'dependency' on the therapist accounts for their apparent reluctance to get better. Or maybe it's just a question of 'inadequate personality'. It is here that one encounters the notion of 'responsibility'.

Views of 'responsibility' in therapy have evolved through a kind of dialectical process, itself shaped by changes and developments in the socio-political context (and associated professional interests) in which the phenomena of and explanations for 'mental disorder' have been set.

In the early 1960s (in Britain), the dominant philosophy in both psychiatric and psychological spheres was crudely mechanistic and 'objective' in the sense beloved of behaviourists. 'Mental illnesses' were indeed illnesses like any other, imposed on the hapless victim through events beyond his or her control and largely devoid of meaning as far as his or her personal life was concerned; or else they were the result of 'maladaptive' habits acquired through more or less accidental processes of conditioning. Alternative views (as for example psychoanalytic ones) were marginal and largely discredited, and treatment approaches relied on the application of medical or psychological techniques based on biological or behavioural assumptions which paid no attention at all to the patient's subjectivity.

In this setting, certainly, patients were not held officially accountable for their difficulties (though the various forms of 'treatment' meted out often contained a distinctly punitive element that, to the reflective onlooker, belied the morally neutral stance of the practitioners). As responsible agent and subject, the individual person was simply an irrelevance.

When, therefore, theoretical innovators arrived on the scene, such as R.D. Laing in psychiatry and Carl Rogers and George Kelly in clinical psychology, their introduction into the picture of notions like meaning, subjectivity and responsibility brought fresh, new perspectives which many of us seized on with relief and enthusiasm. The 'organism' that had been the object of the clinical gaze became a human being whose troubles were to be understood as the product of a particular life.

What has happened over the years is that a mechanistic and objectivist approach to people's distress that, while it didn't overtly blame them, *dehumanised* them, has been replaced by a 'humanist' and 'postmodernist' one that *interiorises* the phenomena of distress and—often explicitly and nearly always tacitly—holds people responsible for them. Even though the pendulum seems to have swung from an almost entirely exterior approach to an almost entirely interior one, the problem of responsibilty has not been solved: formerly we had people for whose condition *nobody* was responsible, while now we have people whose condition is largely if not solely *their own* responsibility. The reason for this is once again to be found in what these two extreme positions have in common: a studied avoidance of the social dimension.

It is true that, as the pendulum began to swing (for example with Laing's work), the social power structure did indeed become visible for a moment, even to the extent of spawning 'radical psychology' movements. However, as far as the mainstream is concerned, the possibility that emotional distress is the upshot of the way we organise our society has never been seriously entertained and at the present time is if anything further than ever from any kind of official recognition. The imputation of responsibility is absolutely central to this state of affairs.

'Responsibility' is, however, not a unitary concept, and is in fact used in a confusing number of overlapping senses, usually depending for their interpretation on the rhetorical ploy the utterer is seeking to adopt. The most frequent everyday use is that of responsibility as blame: 'Who is responsible?' is equivalent to 'Who is to blame?'. This is the sense in which people suffering emotional distress usually understand 'responsibility', and I would maintain that for the most part they are not mistaken in their anticipation that this is how society also understands it in relation to 'psychological disorder'.

Once the concept of responsibility is invoked in this sphere it raises the question of who is to blame for my suffering—I, or someone else? The message of the therapeutic industry has been that the blame lies with the sufferer; it is of course not stated as crudely as this, but is implied in the notion that somehow the individual lacks the moral fibre to face up to his or her difficulties and mobilise the necessary internal resources to deal with them. Most sufferers feel this keenly without any overt prompting from those around them: a guilty sense of weakness and moral inadequacy is one of the most frequent and uncomfortable accompaniments of distress.

With the exception of legal responsibility, which largely concerns the external imposition of clearly defined and codified rules and obligations that, it is assumed, the individual may choose to observe or transgress, 'responsibility' is usually seen as a kind of praiseworthy moral faculty internally available to everyone who is not in some way exceptionally damaged, as for example by brain injury or madness. 'Responsibility' is thus a kind of virtue (closely related to 'will-power') which may be appealed to, a 'sense' which may when necessary be sternly invoked, or a capacity for resolve which may be stiffened through therapeutic intervention.

It is important to note this *virtuous* quality of responsibility, for while it may constitute a mark of maturity and an index of mental 'wellness', it is not usually seen as something beyond the person's power to summon up if absolutely necessary. Only in the most exceptional circumstances will a healthy adult be considered 'not responsible' for his or her actions. The exercise of this kind of virtuous, morally loaded responsibility is often seen as burdensome. To act responsibly is to choose to act with consideration and restraint; to act irresponsibly is take the easier path of selfishness, disobedience, disloyalty.

There is enormous potential here for hypocrisy, sanctimony and manipulation. For when 'responsibility' of the morally virtuous kind is most earnestly advocated, it is usually by the advantaged for the disadvantaged. To say that someone is irresponsible, 'has no will-power', etc., is not to commiserate with them as having been somehow *deprived* of virtue, but at least tacitly to accuse them of wilfully witholding conduct that they could enact if they chose. There is, I suggest, a strong positive correlation between a) the height of the rung occupied on the ladder of power, b) the strength of a sense of personal virtue, and c) the firmness of the conviction that those lower down could and certainly should act more responsibly.

The sense in which therapists and counsellors advocate responsibility for their clients probably derives also from the existential view that, to achieve 'authenticity', a person must embrace the inevitability of their own choice of action: your fate is to be free and no one performs your actions but you. While this view may have the merit of escaping the blind mechanism of orthodox (medical and behavioural) approaches, it rarely manages to avoid the moralism which so easily attends the notion of responsibility, and therapeutic practitioners quickly find themselves in a familiar paradox.

For while they exhort their clients to 'take responsibility' for their lives, they concurrently assure them that they know that 'pull yourself together' is a popular prescription that doesn't work. The therapeutic notion of responsibility, it is implied, is altogether different, more subtle, than crude advice about pulling selves together. The trouble is, though, that in practice there is very little difference between these two approaches, and indeed as far as clients experience them they are virtually identical.

As I have already indicated, to understand why therapists and counsellors have been locked in this contradiction for so long one need look no further than their interests. Quite obviously, they are unable to claim that their influence can reach in any significant way beyond the consulting room, and if they are to justify taking fees for their activities, it simply *must* be the case that clients harbour *within* them the possibility of change. Therapy creates the crucible in which it is forced thereafter to work its magic, and any theoretical consideration of responsibility is inexorably limited to the (supposed) moral resources of the client.

But the paradox of responsibility is escaped easily enough, I believe, if one extends the analysis beyond the walls of the consulting room. For responsibility is inextricably bound up with power, and power is accorded from without, not from within.

People cannot 'pull themselves together' not out of any wilful reluctance to do so, but because the *power* to do so is not available to them. Exactly the same applies to 'responsibility'. I can be held responsible only for what I have the power to do, and if I do indeed have the power to choose, only then can I reasonably be said to be responsible for my choices. No responsibility without power; no power without responsibility. And we are not talking here about 'will-power': the exercise of responsibility in no way depends on the application of any such mysterious internal faculty (see the previous chapter), but rather on the availability of external powers and resources.

Our 'self-as-centre' culture makes it very difficult for us to conceive of responsibility as anything other than the application of personal influence which has its origin entirely within the individual agent. It takes quite an effort of imagination to see the person—as I have suggested (in Chapter Two) we should—as a point in social space-time *through which* powers flow. Though, as an individual, I am indeed that point through which whatever powers and resources available to me may be, so to speak, refracted back into the social world, I certainly did not personally create them out of nothing.

Quite apart from our star-struck admiration of celebrity, we have an enduring cultural tradition of fascination with and deference to power which induces us to see it as an individual quality—even, as I have already suggested, a virtue. We see 'great men' (and sometimes women) as preciously rare phenomena, bestowed upon the world by some nameless providence, and we honour their occurrence with a special kind of awed respect.

While there are clearly aspects of embodiment that contribute to some kinds of exceptional ability—not everyone can be an Olympic athlete—it is altogether an open question whether the kind of admiration we are ready all too often to accord people who find themselves in the position of wielding *social* power is justified by their personal qualities. It takes a Tolstoy (in *War and Peace*) to see through the myth surrounding Napoleon and it is only in retrospect that the absurdity of Hitler's status is revealed.

'The psychology of leaders,' Chomsky writes, 'is a topic of little interest. The institutional factors that constrain their actions and beliefs are what merit attention.'[1] And that is precisely the point: circumstances choose the person, not vice versa. Since circumstances decree that there can be only one leader, we make the mistake of concluding that the leader who emerges—Hitler, say—is unique, either (at the time we adulate him) in his virtue or (after his fall from grace) in his evil. It is, however, the office (and what sustains it) that is unique, not the person. Just look at the politician who is voted from power or the pop star who falls out of the charts—victims of instant ordinariness! Here, before our very eyes, we observe what happens when social power ceases to flow through the embodied locus which constitutes our individuality. In fact, as the cynical manipulators of the popular culture industries well recognise, the 'unique star' can be elevated from a very wide range of very ordinary people, but, having been selected, it takes a rare and exceptionally balanced head for the manufactured celebrity not to believe in his or her own image.

The notion of 'responsibility' lies at the heart of what one might well call our suppression of the social. Whatever it is we seek to understand—ranging from the reasons for personal distress to the 'evil' of spectacular crime or the failure of public servants to avert some social disaster—it is always to an unanalysed and unanalysable individual, internal world (where 'blame' is harboured) that we turn our gaze.

Outrage breaks out in the media with monotonous regularity concerning—just as one example—the death of a child who has been brutally abused and finally killed by its deranged carers. Yet another example of official failure, apparently. Who's to blame here? The doctor who misdiagnosed the child's injuries? Its social worker? The social worker's managers? The police? Dismay is widespread that 'the system' still fails after all the previous enquiries and reports following similar instances.

Almost never does one see in these discussions a cool appraisal of the society in which the unfortunate family was located, of the sheer weight and number of desperate circumstances like these, of the fatigue and overwork of those struggling to operate the underfunded and undervalued public services. No one draws the obvious inference from the dreary repetition of such cases that they are bound to be a regular feature of a society which tolerates such high levels of deprivation. Books like Nick Davies's *Dark Heart,*[2] which take pains to spell out the social conditions of 'evil' are vanishingly rare, and when they do appear seem hardly to be noticed.

This evasion of the obvious—that it is the way our society is organised and structured that constitutes the main source of our difficulties—is understandable only in terms of the extent of the powers which are deployed to maintain it. This can be seen very clearly in current political discourse.

As essential cogs in the vast economic machine designed to extract profit for the minority at the top of the social pyramid, politicians have an important role in representing disadvantage as personal moral failure. How wittingly they perform this role is open to question but, as a matter of 'commentary', a question of little interest. The distal pressures on the advocates of the 'third way' to reinforce an interiorised view of responsibility are enormous.

Policies of 'naming and shaming', the imputation that inadequacies in health and education are somehow due to the unwillingness of individual teachers, doctors, nurses, social workers, etc., to apply themselves to the full, linkage of 'rights' with 'responsibilities', and so on, all help to constitute the political paradox that those in the position (or so it would seem) of being most able to shape distal influences, expend the greatest energy in representing them as proximal (indeed internal).

In typically Orwellian manner, the conditions in which responsibility can and should be exercised become inverted, and 'third way' politicians preach responsibility for those who have no power while utterly disregarding the duties to society of those who have. Entire communities (miners, steelworkers) can be thrown on the social scrapheap in the interests of profit, and the only official talk of 'responsibility' is for those whose lives have been shattered to accept whatever scraps are thrown to them and sort themselves out as best they can without disturbing the peace

In fact, of course, national politics does not so much exercise power as serve it. Where multinational capital dominates, the local political role becomes that of obscuring the true sources of power and the effects these have on the objective and subjective well-being of the citizenry. 'Politics' becomes a form of *management* that itself actually destroys the public space in which political activity can take place. Our possibility of playing an active part in influencing those social structures that ultimately impinge intimately on our lives is whittled away to nothing, while our relative immiseration becomes internalised as personal fault.

Poverty, for example, is represented in 'third way' politics not as an evil that causes social disintegration and personal emotional damage, but as an unwarrantable 'excuse' for individual moral failure. The crumbling of public services, increase in crime, etc., are represented as the result of the incompetence, intransigence and irresponsibility of public-sphere workers and of the 'evil' apparently endemic in the 'criminal element' of society.[3]

When it comes to trying to decide what people can be held accountable for and what not, the subjective sense of 'responsibility' is almost entirely unreliable. Everyone is familiar with liars and self-deceivers who claim that something was not their fault when it obviously was. What presents more of a challenge to psychological understanding is those people who claim and feel responsibility for things that are in fact obviously outside their control. Perhaps it is the greater authenticity of the over-conscientious person compared with the deceiver that gives us a clue as to why any 'internal' account of responsibility is invalid. The conscience, after all, does not lie: it reports (commentates) faithfully enough on how it feels to be the instrument of wrongdoing. But, as is clearly demonstrated by those in whom it is over-developed, the conscience can be *mistaken*. What it is mistaken about is not the *feeling* of responsibility, but the *origins* (or possibly the definition) of the 'wrongdoing'.

It is the *feeling* of responsibility (conscience) that the powerful seek to exploit in others in order to divert attention from the actual (distal) *causes* of their discomfort. I am host to the powers that flow through me and, if I'm honest (authentic), I cannot deny the sense of ownership that they create in their passage. The person who *does* seek to deny this sense of ownership, possibly by claiming 'It wasn't me', or 'It's not my fault, I had a terrible childhood', etc., is no doubt being inauthentic. Though inauthenticity can indeed become elevated to rank bad faith (witness for example Toscanini's excusing an assault on a fellow musician on the grounds that he was 'in the grip of genius'!), it is not *necessarily* inaccurate from a causal perspective. When it comes to 'responsibility', we attach as a society much greater weight to authenticity than to accuracy.

For the purposes of understanding how and why people experience and act in the world as they do, and what freedom they may have to act otherwise, the concept of 'responsibility' has become virtually useless. What we need is a psychology that switches its attention from a metaphorical 'inner world' to try instead to elaborate the ways in which powerful influences in the external environment of social space-time serve to liberate or enslave us, as well as to shape our consciousness of ourselves. As things are, it is not at all clear how far individuals are able to marshal and control the influences that flow through them. Furthermore, in our attempt to understand the processes involved we are constantly misled by the assumption that our commentary refers directly to them.

Notes

1. Chomsky, Noam. 1989. *Necessary Illusions*. Pluto Press, p. 19.

2. Davies, Nick. 1998. *Dark Heart: The shocking truth about hidden Britain*. Vintage.

3. For an effective counter to this latter tendency see Elie Godsi's *Violence and Society: Making sense of madness and badness*. 2004. PCCS Books.

5

What Then Must We Do?

That is the question that Leo Tolstoy, having surveyed the misery of the ordinary Russian people, tried to answer in 1886. It is also the question that people pose—often somewhat resentfully—when confronted by the kind of objections to the social and psychological status quo that I have raised in these pages. 'It's all very well to criticise, but have you got any better ideas…?'

The role of critic in the psychological world tends not to be a comfortable one, and invites various dismissive diagnoses from those who seem to feel affronted: 'pessimist', 'depressive', 'arrogant', 'cynic', and so on. It is not to avoid these diagnoses that I attempt an answer to the 'What must we do?' question here—I shall probably not escape them come what may. I merely want to demonstrate that an answer is not difficult to find. The difficulty, as the oblivion into which Tolstoy's wonderful book has sunk demonstrates so well, is in putting any answer into practice.

We are faced at the societal level with exactly the same problem that faces the client of well-conducted psychotherapy: we can see clearly enough the events—among them our own actions—that have led to our predicament, but the means of rectifying them are still beyond our reach. As I have argued elsewhere,[1] tragedy offers a far better model for human distress than does the fatuous optimism of magical voluntarism: however hard we struggle to rectify the errors that insight reveals, we are still overtaken by their consequences.

And so the 'answers' that I consider below are not given in the expectation that they are to be easily achieved, or indeed achieved at all. Perhaps, at most, they may help to retain a kind of hope.

In keeping with the 'proximal–distal' dimension that I have used to consider the causes of distress, so also the implications for what we should do may be categorised according to the readiness of their availability to us as individuals. There are, it seems to me, four spheres in which action necessary to redress the difficulties identified in the previous pages of this work may conceivably be taken. Ranging from the proximal to the distal, they are the clinical, scientific, philosophical and ethical/political spheres. I hope it goes without saying that in what follows I am not pretending to offer an exhaustive analysis of what may be possible, but merely picking out some of the more important issues that suggest themselves for our attention.

Implications for 'clinical' practice

We cannot, I think, escape the clinic. Although it is almost certainly not the most appropriate site in which to address the kinds of psychological distress and suffering that afflict people in present-day society, there is no other that is obviously more appropriate. Although the long-term answers to those of our woes that are potentially amenable to influence may lie much more at the distal reaches of social organisation, it is (as clinicians are the first to point out) still *individuals* who suffer and seek some remedy to their pain. It would be a callous society indeed that stood back and offered them nothing just because nothing much is likely to provide any real 'cure' at the personal level. It is incumbent on us to do what we can, even if we cannot do much. In a fractured, largely urban society in which, thankfully, religion no longer plays a significant role, the clinic, in one form or another, is the place people will turn to when in difficulty, and it is for the foreseeable future in the clinic that we shall probably be doing the little that we can. As it is, however, the clinic is profoundly inadequate for the task at hand.

No one is more aware of this inadequacy than those who encounter the clinic—whether as practitioners, consumers or simply observers—and are able and willing to reflect on their experience of and role within it. For counsellors and therapists trapped within the horizon set by their immediate interests, such reservations about the scope of psychological help are likely to be angrily dismissed as 'nihilism'; but there are signs of an emergent critique of therapy that acknowledges the *modesty* of the therapeutic contribution—particularly in relation to its neglect of social factors—while at the same time offering a persuasive defence of its practice.[2] While this literature is scattered and shows—mercifully—no sign of coalescing into any kind of unified movement or school, what its contributors tend to share is a recognition of the 'ordinary' humanity of the therapeutic relationship and its role as a source of solidarity rather than a technology of 'change'.

For my part, I would emphasise the following as legitimate concerns for the psychology of distress:

- *Demystification.* Although itself not a concept taken up by counsellors and psychotherapists in their theoretical reflections, 'demystification' describes quite well what the best of them spend much of their time doing in practice. For it is indeed the case that people seeking therapy often start out with very little idea about what is causing their troubles. Conventional therapies spend a great deal of time in what one might call the demystification of the proximal sphere, i.e. unpicking with clients the events and relationships in their immediate experience which give rise to all the phenomena of psychological distress, self-accusation and self-deception that are familiar to most practitioners (I have tried to describe the foremost among these in *How to Survive Without Psychotherapy.)*[3] Elsewhere I have called this process 'clarification', and it is perhaps the most developed of the three principal planks of therapy (the other two being 'comfort' and 'encouragement'); that is to say, it is the process that therapists of all schools spend most time thinking and writing about, and attempting to teach. Insofar as there can be said to be 'skills' of therapy and counselling, the arts of listening carefully and helping to clear ways through people's confusion probably can be developed through guided practice, and hence tend to form the core of most schemes of 'training'.

However, having, so to speak, cleared the conceptual undergrowth obscuring the client's view of his or her immediate predicament (so as to achieve 'insight'), most approaches to therapy consider that the work of clarification is done and that it is now up to the clients themselves to switch on their 'responsibility' and put matters right in ways that I have suggested in earlier pages are quite likely impossible. The notion that a 'clinical' predicament could (through 'outsight') be demystified to the point of showing that there is *nothing* a client could do about it precisely *because* it is not his or her fault, but the outcome of distal influences over which s/he can have no control, is unacceptable to most therapists not because it is unreasonable but, as I have already pointed out, because it is from a professional point of view extremely inconvenient. From the client's point of view, however, it need not be inconvenient at all, but constitute rather the lifting of a heavy burden of moral apprehension, if not outright guilt, that was completely unmerited. The aim of therapy then becomes to clarify what it is *not,* as well as what it is, possible for individuals to do to influence their circumstances and, given the limited powers available to most of us to act upon our world, the most 'therapeutic' outcome may well be achieved by the former.

Such an undertaking leads to a very different kind of dialogue from that characteristic of conventional therapy. Rather than there being a progressive emphasis on the 'inside', culminating in the patient's assumption of responsibility for a moral universe of which s/he is supposedly the author, there is likely to be a literal process of 'enlightenment' in which the person is released from all kinds of mystified responsibilities and helped to see him- or herself as embodied and located within an external reality highly resistant to individual influence and totally impervious to wishfulness. The implications of such a dialogue are indeed radical—even, given the nature of current Western society, subversive—but they may still be therapeutic.

- *Rescuing subjectivity*. I have already written in Chapter Three of the ways in which contemporary consumer capitalism turns us inside out as well as outside in (i.e. hopelessly confuses our public and private lives), disembodies, dislocates and dissociates us in such a way that we have no clear idea of what legitimately constitutes our selves in relation to others.

  An obvious implication of this observation *at the theoretical level* is that we need to re-embody, relocate and re-associate the human subject such that s/he is lifted out of the realm of ideality (see Fig. 2.1) and placed in a proper relation with the body, the world and other people (with all the limitations on magical voluntarism that that implies). This, no doubt, should be the work of academic writers and researchers who take reality and society seriously, and there are encouraging signs that such work, particularly in the form of 'critical realism' is gaining ground in clinical awareness.[4]

  What we may be able to do *in practice* is probably more limited. While therapy as such has little or no power to reconstruct the kind of public space that would support, value and make use of our subjective experience (this being essentially a political matter), it may at least work to undo some of the damage that its essentially disciplinary ideology has done in calling into question the very foundations of our sense of personhood. The moral and aesthetic strictures lying at the heart of so much 'humanist' therapy need to give way to a recognition that we are, as subjective individuals, *all* uniquely, chaotically and (at least potentially) creatively *peculiar.*

  As a matter of fact I suspect that in practice (as opposed to their official pronouncements) many counsellors and therapists adopt an approach to their clients which affirms rather than subverts their vulnerable subjectivity (this, no doubt is why therapy is so often seen as a preferable alternative to the 'medical model' of psychiatry). Nevertheless, this is not a securely established aspect of therapy in general, and far too many clients will have experienced an increasing rather than a lessening strain on their subjective experience of self as the result of therapy.

  But what does it mean to 'affirm vulnerable subjectivity'?

- *The rehabilitation of character.* The notion of 'change' lies at the heart of virtually all approaches to psychotherapy and counselling. At first glance it seems, furthermore, self-evident that it should. Asked what it is that should change as the result of therapy, most practitioners would, I suspect, refer to some aspect of the client's 'self', i.e., something inside the person. At one extreme this might be, for example, aspects of a hypothetical construct like 'the unconscious'; at the other, the internal cognitive processes that are taken to control behaviour. It is this insistence on change that in my view tends to cancel out many of the otherwise valuable insights that therapists have articulated over the years. People are not allowed to be themselves.

    Take as an instance of this the 'client-centred' approach of Carl Rogers. As Rogers's work gained in influence at about the middle of the twentieth century, it did indeed bring with it a great sense of liberation: much of the grim, covert moralism of 'dynamic' psychotherapy seemed to fall away, and the emphasis Rogers placed on 'unconditional positive regard' and 'empathy' seemed to allow subjects to escape the yoke of therapeutic discipline and, precisely, come to be themselves.

    But, as the professions of therapy and counselling burgeoned, 'positive regard' turned out not to be unconditional, and empathy to be not so much an end as a means. For these constructs were treated as merely *instrumental* in the altogether superordinate task of bringing about change. The upshot of this is to place a new burden on patients, for they are freed from an external therapeutic discipline (mediated by 'interpretation', 'the 'analysis of the transference', etc.) only to have to repay the warmth and empathy of their therapist by successfully changing them*selves*. The Rogerian counsellor is not *just* warm and empathic: the warmth and empathy carries with it an expectation—all too easily turning to an obligation—to *change*.

    Much of the time, however, for reasons dealt with at length in earlier pages, change is precisely what clients cannot do: not because of incompetence or ill will, but because the powers by which change could be effected are, quite literally, beyond them. To all the other senses of inadequacy and guilt that they may be carrying, then, is added the guilt of being unable to reward their counsellor's kindness with an appropriate therapeutic adjustment of self.

    The answer to this dilemma, I believe, is to remove from an otherwise benign emphasis on acceptance and empathy their element of instrumentality. They should be, simply, ends in themselves. The best word I can think of for an appropriate, non-instrumental approach for therapists and counsellors to take to their clients is *compassion*: not so different from 'empathy', perhaps, but a little warmer, recognising not so much that it is necessary to stand in the other's shoes, but that we *already are* in each other's shoes. If pricked, we bleed.

What clients have to change, if they can, is not their selves, but their world, and in their attempts to do that both they and we have no realistic alternative to accepting that they are who they are. I, you, everybody is not so much a 'personality', with all the assumptions that tends to bring of a modular self to which potential structural adjustments of various kinds may be made, as a *character*, a body inscribed by its experience of the world, indelibly expert in its own idiosyncrasy. We may *feel with* others whose predicaments form no part of our own experience, but such compassion need bring with it neither the wish nor the hope that they should change. Images of suffering demand not that the sufferer changes him- or herself, but that the suffering should be relieved. The starving child needs food, not moral uplift.[5]

The appropriate role for therapeutic psychology is to record, celebrate and wonder at the extraordinary diversity of human character and to reject immediately any notion it may be tempted to conceive of making moulds for people. We are *really* not there to judge or shape people, and we need nurse no secret agenda for change. Such change as therapists and their clients may pursue together has no need of mystery, nor even delicacy, but is a down-to-earth matter of what powers are available to the person to make a difference. And if the person, as is often the case, can do nothing, the compassionate acceptance of who they are may still be a comfort.

- *Reinstating the environment.* There is no reason why 'clinical' psychology should be seen as synonymous with therapy. Indeed, it is only in relatively recent times—particularly with the rise of the 'dynamic' therapies of the twentieth century—that the doctoring of the self has come to be seen as the principal business of psychology. The focal concern of psychology with the making of individual subjectivity in no way implies that subjectivity is necessarily *self*-made. Personhood, along with the subjective awareness of it, is the outcome of an interaction of a *body* with a *world*, and it therefore behoves the psychologist to pay careful attention to the constraints and influences of both .

  As is the case with the emerging discipline of 'community psychology',[6] it makes as much sense now as it did to Plato to consider the ways in which individuals are shaped by their environments, and to distinguish environmental influences that are benign from those that are malign.

If this seems entirely obvious, it is salutary to remember that the whole thrust of 'therapy', and much of the weight of 'evidence' from social psychology, has been to suggest that the environment does not have a defining influence on individual psychology, and that not only can people somehow choose whether to be influenced by it or not, but that pretty well any damage done can be repaired. Earnest debates take place as to whether, for example, poverty and unemployment, loss, brutality and violence contribute to mental disorder, crime, and so on. The fact that human beings are complex, resourceful and resilient means that simple cause-and-effect answers to such questions are not unequivocally demonstrable, and so it is easy to conclude that the pain and havoc wreaked by the ills of society are actually factors of, for instance, weak or vulnerable 'personalities' rather than of the ills themselves. This answer is of course exactly what is required by a global, corporate plutocracy that depends for its survival on the unremitting exploitation of a mass of 'consumers' who must a) be stuffed to bursting point with rubbish, and b) be rendered as far as possible incapable of accurately criticising their condition.

But the relation between environmental influence and personal psychology is complex not because it is mediated by some indefinable aspect of the 'human spirit', but because environmental influence is in itself far more complex than we have hitherto considered. Because psychology (and especially therapeutic psychology) has been so preoccupied with supposedly interior factors of motivation and cognition, etc., its considerations of environmental influences has frequently been extraordinarily crude and casual—to the extent that it could be argued, for example, that siblings share a 'similar environment' or that the influence of TV violence could be measured by showing violent cartoons to toddlers and observing their behaviour immediately afterwards.

In fact, of course, people know perfectly well that huge advantages are to be gained from occupancy of favourable environments, and the more they have been beneficiaries of such environments, the better they know it. Moralistic homilies and visions of a compensatory after-life are strictly for the masses. The occupants of corporate boardrooms and big country mansions pay unwavering attention to, for example, the kinds of educational establishment attended by their offspring and the quality of 'lifestyle' they submit themselves to.

How environmental influence works, how it interacts with embodiment, how some social relations become crucial while others glance off apparently unnoticed, constitute questions of enormous subtlety and difficulty and provide material for generations of study.

This is, furthermore, a perfectly proper study for 'clinicians'. Rather than attempting to peer into the murky depths of a metaphorical psychic interior, populated only by the hypothetical constructs of our own imagination, we need to get down to the much more difficult and demanding task of trying to tease out the ways in which environmental influences combine and interact to shape our subjectivity.

Care does have to be taken, however, that we do not allow our 'clinical' and scientific interest to expropriate the political role of the citizen. Some 'critical psychologists' show an alarming tendency to professionalise politics in exactly the potentially disabling way that Ivan Illich identified in other professions.[7] For example, in their book extolling the virtues of 'critical psychology',[8] Prilleltensky and Nelson seem possessed by overweening hubris in their vision of what professional 'critical psychologists' can achieve in the pursuit of the public good.[9] We would do better, I think, to bear in mind Russell Jacoby's observation that the point is:

> ... to realise to what extent even the most extended therapy remains therapy: a choice in how to treat the individual that leaves untouched the social roots. In that sense there is no such activity as radical therapy— there is only therapy and radical politics. Need it be said? There is no shame in aiding the victims, the sick, the damaged, the down-and-out. If mental illness and treatment are class illness and treatment, there is much to be done within this reality. But the reformation of the social reality is another project, which if it is not utterly distinct from therapy, is not to be confused with it.[10]

Scientific implications

I don't want to get into an argument about what does and does not constitute 'science', and I certainly don't want to align myself with the narrow Anglo-American scientistic orthodoxy that tends to get dismissed by its opponents as 'positivistic'. But neither do I want to subscribe to the neo-Romantic position often taken up by anti-science, in which rhyme is preferred to reason.

What seems to me important, for 'clinical' psychology anyway, is what I take to be the broad project of science rather than the particular content of its methodology. By this I mean a commitment to achieving and communicating an understanding of the world and its occupants that is based on experience, reasoned argument, painstaking and sceptical checking and, ultimately, an appropriate (though very rarely total) degree of consensus (Habermas's 'communicative action').[11] It seems to me that this process is likely to be essentially materialist and realist, though of course critically so.

The integrity and value of science in this sense depends on its being unconstrained and unperverted by special interests or by the kind of Authority that forms itself into a dogmatic ruling orthodoxy. And that kind of freedom is of course precisely what, in our neck of the social-scientific woods, we have not got. What has come to be put forward as 'scientific' in clinical psychology and psychotherapy is a set of dogmas that is shaped and maintained almost exclusively by interest in relation to the ruling discourses of power and aimed resolutely at obscuring the causes and consequences of emotional and psychological distress.

I have already identified the two main sources of interest involved in this state of affairs. The first is the proximal interest of clinicians who, whether consciously or not, perceive their livelihood to depend ultimately on their personal ability to bring about cure (though they may find a more intellectually diplomatic word for it). This is the source of interest that guides much of the research activity and clinical case discussion in the literature on therapy and counselling. It makes sure that only certain kinds of question are asked and only certain kinds of 'finding' considered relevant: questions about therapeutic *technique* presuppose clear-cut answers that, when they are not forthcoming, are taken to indicate simply the need for more research.

The second, more distal, influence is broadly political, and seeks to maintain a fiction of personal psychopathology as the explanation for mental 'disorders'. The drive, for example, for 'evidence-based practice' in 'mental health' services is imposed by central management diktat and countenances only research projects that conform to a primitive set of quasi-medical assumptions dressed up as 'science'. Inspired by Fordist and Taylorist principles (i.e. the conveyor-belt, deliberately depersonalised and managerially controlled methods of production developed towards the beginning of the twentieth century), the Business model of knowledge which has come to prevail in the last twenty years is technicist and crudely pragmatic. It assumes that knowledge production is achieved by posing appropriate sets of designer questions and must be directed and controlled by management. Once produced, knowledge is to be transmitted thereafter by means of off-the-shelf 'training' modules.

This approach to the managerially directed division of labour in 'science', whereby centrally determined questions are farmed out to technicians for a kind of algorithmic 'research' process yielding packaged knowledge that, in turn, is further disseminated by operatives versed in the techniques of training, rules out just about everything that is creative, intelligent and worthwhile in scientific discovery and teaching. For these latter are processes that take place at the very forefront of human endeavour (i.e. are not manageable 'skills') and depend for their significance and fruitfulness on qualities of understanding and enquiry that are not specifiable technically in advance. The kinds of flexibility and resourcefulness, sensitivity and intelligence that are the hallmarks of, for example, good scientists and teachers cannot be contained within a packaged 'spec' of the kind so beloved of business managers (the myth of specifiability is a core feature of Business culture), but are the result of a kind of nurturing husbandry of inquisitiveness and creativity whose results can be only hoped for, not guaranteed.[12]

By deliberately excluding the kind of intellectual originality and adventurousness that is characteristic of real achievement in the sciences as much as the arts, Business may well protect itself from unwanted surprises, but it does so at the expense of producing a dumbed-down, uncritical environment that is deadeningly third rate, uncreative, and ultimately (because essentially stupefied and imperceptive) profoundly ineffective.

Just as one example, the corruption of science by business interest in the pharmaceutical industry could almost stand as a microcosm of current society. Impecunious scientists whose public funding has been withdrawn are induced to have articles published in learned journals under their name, but which have in fact been written by ghost writers in the pay of the drug companies.[13] In this way an appearance of independent *evidence* is used to create a spurious *authority* to underpin *make-believe*.

Though no doubt intellectually demanding in many respects, the scientific method is at its best the least coercive as well as the most accurate way we have of establishing what is—while acknowledging the limitations of these concepts—'real' and 'true'. The effectiveness of the scientific method, fundamentally libertarian at its core, is not lost on those wishing to co-opt it in their interest; but to do so they have, of course, to pervert it.

At the crudest level there is simply the possibility of fiddling the figures—an approach widely adopted in recent years by, in particular, governments who wish to 'demonstrate' that what isn't the case, is (e.g. the ceaseless manipulation of employment and other statistics). Beyond this, however, is the far more insidious intrusion of corrupting power into the scientific community itself. Instead of 'the evidence' flowing from the unconstrained agreement of unbiased observers struggling in good faith to arrive at the most objective assessment possible, it becomes a kind of bludgeon with which to silence precisely those same observers. Scientific procedure and activity becomes reified as 'the science' (as in 'doing the science'), the 'quality' of which is established by authoritative pronouncement rather than by free, on-going debate within the length and breadth of the scientific community.

The social sciences are particularly vulnerable to this kind of corruption, nowhere more obviously than in the case of the evaluation of the effectiveness of psychotherapy. The interests of a booming industry combine with those of a handful of academic 'authorities' such that the latter use their status within the system to *assert* the effectiveness of therapy, basing their 'argument' on a tiny (and entirely questionable) handful of studies and in the face of mountains of counter-evidence which have accumulated over decades.[14] 'Scientific' debate, in such circumstances, becomes an adversarial contest in which 'evidence' is treated like a kind of rhetorical football, depending for its credibility on the relative status and visibility of the academic players.

This kind of corrupted 'evidence' is not the only basis on which professionals and academics seek to ground their authority. As the reaction to 'positivist' science has taken hold—in Britain, at least—over the past couple of decades or so there has been an increasing tendency within the social sciences to resort to what Philo and Miller[15] call 'obfuscation and abstraction' as a kind of indirect authority for assent. There has always been a tendency on the intellectual left—particularly perhaps among Continental thinkers—to take complexity and opacity as an indication of profundity and significance (in the psychotherapy field one thinks instantly of Jacques Lacan and his minions). This can quite easily turn into a kind of intellectual terrorism where, for example, angry but obscure 'theorists' descend on conference audiences to harangue them into submission with the sheer virtuosity of their mind-numbing (though essentially meaningless) intellectual gymnastics.

Though very far from being concerned with evidence of any kind, successful proponents of the authority-through-obscurity school share with scientists of the authority-through-status school a kind of meta-status of authority-through-celebrity. It is hardly surprising that in a society obsessed with celebrity, knowledge eventually becomes the preserve of a kind of Olympian priesthood of 'names' who circulate endlessly around the higher-brow media, pronouncing with absolute confidence on matters for which there is in fact no evidence at all.

The outcome of this state of affairs is disastrous, for the process whereby we arrive as a society at objective judgements about reality has become corrupted and rendered untrustworthy at its very heart. Scientific argument becomes a contest of authority based on status (a concept *fundamentally* inimical to the scientific method) and ordinary people understandably turn from a power-ridden perversion of 'objectivity' to essentially magical systems which, though equally if not more misleading, seem at least subjectively satisfying.

As far as research in 'clinical' psychology is concerned, we need to recognise that (as, no doubt, in many other areas) no further progress will be made until we have re-established an environment for theoretical speculation and practical enquiry that is both independent and secure. That is to say, the discovery and development of knowledge (recognising and communicating what is true about the world) is completely inimical to the play of interest and must, as far as is humanly possible, be separated from it. The one-dimensional culture of the corporate plutocracy, interested only in profit, is incapable of producing the conditions in which intellectual pursuits flourish. For the kinds of unconditional patronage and guaranteed independence necessary will not only be seen ideologically as needlessly wasteful and unacceptably out of managerial control, but would in fact inevitably constitute a threat to the corporate regime itself. As soon as the cultural unidimensionality of Business is shattered by the introduction of non-bottom-line dimensions, it finds itself vulnerable to orders of criticism that threaten its very survival.

Business is definitely not out to further the disinterested pursuit of scientific evidence. The principal alternative open to it is, as we have seen, the development of increasingly convoluted systems of make-believe to run alongside the extremely banal technological processes of knowledge production that are managerially controllable.

Philosophical implications[16]

The great paradox of the 'linguistic turn' that has excited so many psychologists within recent years is that, at the same time as helping to construct a mythical, essentially interior world of 'discourse', it radically undermined our ability to talk about a real, exterior world. In this state of affairs the philosophical task becomes that of rehabilitating the concept of truth, which in turn means deconstructing constructivism! In this we may look for help once again to 'critical realism' (see previous section).

There can be no doubt that language is of the first importance in the formation of human conduct and society. But this does not mean that language is generative of reality itself. The over-excited embrace (and often only rudimentary understanding) in broadly 'therapeutic' circles of notions of 'discourse', 'narrative', etc., claiming their origin mainly in the writings of French post-structuralists such as Foucault, Derrida and Lyotard, has resulted, as I noted in Chapter One, in an almost psychotic disregard of the real circumstances of people's lives.

Of course words do not directly reflect an incontrovertible reality or 'hold a mirror up to Nature';[17] *of course* language can never give direct access to Truth. And of course language is absolutely essential to our understanding of and interaction with the world and each other. But this does not invest language with some kind of magical power of creation in which it brings worlds into being. Certainly language is the principal medium of persuasion, but it persuades by pointing to something other than itself, something that *is the case* rather than something that is merely *said*.

It is easy to see how we can be misled by our linguistic ability into investing it with magical power; but only the machinations of power, surely, can explain the extent to which the world has come to be presented as dematerialised at the highest intellectual levels. Foucault spoke, after all, of the 'discourse of power', not the power of discourse, and yet it is this misconstruction which seems to have gripped the imagination of the 'constructivists'. Language does not *describe* reality, they say, in contemptuous dismissal of the 'grand narratives of the past'. No, but neither does it bring it into being.

Language allows us to place our experience at a distance from us, to hypostatise and manipulate it. Otherwise, we could only *live* our experience—or be lived by it, rather in the manner of dreaming. Inevitably, we are constantly tempted to believe in the actuality of our imaginings (which is why scientific enquiry has to be so sceptical and so painstaking), but when we take imagination as definitive of reality (or alternative realities), we have sunk into collective madness.

It is in the interest of any powerful minority that has been able to shape society to its own considerable material benefit, and at the cost of depriving the majority, to obscure not only the processes by which it has achieved its position but also the very nature of reality itself, particularly the significance of people's experience of pain. There is enormous scope for such obfuscation in the time-honoured and entirely familiar ideological and rhetorical manoeuvres ('spin' and PR) that aim at convincing us that black is white. But to insert at the highest levels of philosophical thought the premise that there is no such thing as reality is a coup indeed.

While we may agree that in the past a too heavy-handed positivist authority attempted to claim a special relationship with Truth that allowed no use of linguistic concepts other than its own (i.e. that language could indeed be used to describe an independent reality), we need to recapture a view of language as *articulating* our relations with the world *as best we can*. We can in this way acknowledge that any form of 'ultimate' reality must always remain a mystery beyond our grasp, but that that does not mean there is no such thing as reality. Some things are more real, some statements more true, than others. Reality is sensed in embodied experience before it is articulated in words—that is to say, it is rooted in our subjectivity—and what we *say* needs always to be checked against other kinds of evidence, including where necessary every other possible intimation we may have of our living existence in material reality.

Psychology, I often feel, has neglected the nature of our attachment to the world. Even more fundamental than our relations within society—and certainly more fundamental than the creations of our imagination—is a rootedness in the physical environment encountered by us as infants as we taste, smell, feel, hear and see ourselves into existence. Of course the world cannot be detached in our awareness from what we—and others—make of it, but nevertheless the demands on us of physical reality are, ultimately, uncompromising. The entire project of mankind has, after all, been to understand and elaborate the nature of the world and our place within it. It may be that we need to move on from psychology's preoccupation with meaning-systems (ideality); not, certainly, to a kind of retro-naïve realism, but to the next turn of a dialectical enquiry into truth that anchors us once again in something beyond our *selves*.

I have often wondered whether the rock-bottom basis of a secure subject might be traced to his or her passionate embrace, from the very first moments of existence, of the world as physical environment. It is as if the infant is presented with a choice: to accept the evidence of its senses, or to bend to the demands of ideological power. Ideally, of course, powerful others (in particular parents) will help the infant interpret and elaborate its experience in ways that are as consistent with reality as the best understandings of the time allow. But often they do not, so that the infant is faced at the very outset of its existence with the dilemma that the Inquisition forced on Galileo much later in his life: whether to abide by the truth and court furious oppression, or earn a quieter life by abandoning it in favour of permissible make-believe.

What prompts what will seem to some, I'm sure, such wild speculation, is my observation over the years of people who have clung on to an obstinate— indeed ultimately unshakeable—trust in their own judgement *no matter what* censure and punishment are brought to bear on them. Such people (I think of them as heroes) are, to be sure, few and far between, and I have puzzled endlessly over what could make such a stance in the world possible. It has only recently occurred to me that this may not so much be a relationship with a special *person* as the relationship with *the world* itself: as if by some miracle of personal history the penny dropped right at the outset for *truth* rather than *authority*. What a profoundly liberating possibility that would be!

Ethical/political implications

Let us not mince matters:

> War and globalisation go hand in hand, leading, in the post-Cold War era, to the destruction of countries and the impoverishment of hundreds of millions of people. In turn, this global economic system is marked by an unprecedented concentration of private wealth. The institutions of war, police repression and economic management interface with one another. NATO is not only in liaison with the Pentagon and the CIA; it also has contacts with the IMF and the World Bank. In turn, the Washington-based international financial bureaucracy, responsible for imposing deadly "economic medicine" on developing countries has close ties to the Wall Street financial establishment.
>
> The powers behind this system are those of the global banks and financial institutions, the military-industrial complex, the oil and energy

giants, the biotech conglomerates and the powerful media and communications giants, which fabricate the news and overtly distort the course of world events. In turn, the police apparatus represses, in the name of "Western democracy", all forms of dissent and critique of the dominant neoliberal ideology.

This "false consciousness" which pervades our societies, prevents critical debate and masks the truth. Ultimately, this false consciousness precludes a collective understanding of the workings of a World economic and political system, which destroys people's lives. The only promise of global capitalism is a World of landless farmers, shuttered factories, jobless workers and gutted social programs with "bitter economic medicine" under the WTO and the IMF constituting the only prescription.

The New World Order is based on the "false consensus" of Washington and Wall Street, which ordains the "free market system" as the only possible choice on the fated road to a "global prosperity".

Michel Chossudovsky[18]

The alternative to a soulless neo-capitalism that tries to bury its rapacious self-interest behind a rationalist—and pitiless—technology requires a revival of our moral sense.

It is inconceivable that emotional suffering could be banished from our lives. Being human entails suffering. At the same time, there can be little doubt that a rearrangement of the ways in which we act towards each other could bring about a very significant lessening in the degree of emotional pain and anguish that has become so commonplace in our society that it is barely noticed.

An ethical vision of peace, justice and freedom is not hard to establish; the landscape of Eden is easily recognised. What is not easy to understand and resist are the many ways in which the means of achieving that vision are concealed and obscured.

Morality arises through the experience of a *common* humanity and its affirmation in the face of power. Morality is not an individual, but a social matter; it makes demands upon us which extend beyond our finite, individual lives. It is about resisting those forces which seek to drive wedges between us in order that some may feel and claim to be more human than others.

Our common humanity rests upon our common embodiment. We are all made in exactly the same way. We all suffer in the same way. Most immoral enterprises seek in one way or another to deny this truth and to justify the greater suffering of the oppressed or exploited on the grounds of their being 'different' in some way—physically, racially, psychologically, genetically, and so on. Absolute, self-conscious immorality, on the other hand, makes use of its knowledge of our common embodiment to inflict maximum pain and threat: the torturer does unto others as he would not have done to himself, and the terrorist, choosing victims at random, implicitly acknowledges the equivalence of all people.

The history of the 'civilised' world is one in which powerful minorities have sought (ever more successfully) to impose and exploit conditions of slavery on an impoverished majority. This is necessarily always an *immoral* undertaking, because it denies the continuity of humanity between slave and master while seeking ideologically to obscure that denial.[19]

At the turn of the twenty-first century there seems to be no moral guidance to point a way out of our predicament. The moral voice, stripped of authority, has been drowned out. God is well and truly dead; the Market has triumphed; only the fittest shall survive. Can there be a moral counter to the new Business barbarism?

One problem is that, unlike the kinds of arguments that establish scientific knowledge, moral arguments are not progressive and cumulative, nor are they ever conclusive. Moral argument and social critique constitute a running battle with ruling power, and even though they may be dealing with eternal truths, they will never find a form in which these can be asserted once and for all; the best they can hope for is to find ever new ways of reformulating and restating their insights such that brakes are applied to the ever-expanding ambitions of self-interested power.

A further difficulty is that, insofar as they are successful, moral argument and praxis will be corrupted and co-opted in the interests of power. Christ's message becomes 'The Church'. Because power is power, it holds all the cards, and will *never* be defeated—only impeded. Perhaps Marx's greatest mistake was to assume that capitalism contained the seeds of its own downfall. Seemingly he hadn't conceived of movable goalposts.

For anyone hoping to win the moral high ground once and for all on the basis of a knock-down argument or a conclusive act of rebellion, the inevitable dominance of a corrupt and corrupting power is likely to be a cause of despair. For such a person the insights into venality, stupidity and corruption of, say, a Swift, turn to absolute cynicism rather than merely profound disillusion. For the over-optimistic, not only are illusions destroyed, but idealism too is crushed.

Illusions and ideals

But there is a big difference between illusions and ideals. The loss of illusion is a necessary process on the painful road of enlightenment; the loss of ideals is spiritual death. The only redeeming prospect is that, unlike bodily death, spiritual death need not be final. Spirit is not a personal possession, but a property of common humanity; it does not die with the individual body, but is in a completely literal sense immortal. Resurrection is possible.

Ideals are in this age poorly understood. People are clear enough about goals, objectives and 'targets', but moral purposes which are *designedly* unachievable faze the Business mind. Ideals are not just unlikely to be realised— by their very nature they can *never* be realised. Nevertheless, their existence is what makes life worth living. The disenchanted world in which the Terminator stalks, stripped to its bare steel bones of all pity and compassion, will find its re-enchantment only through a revival of idealism.

Thus, the essential moral insight is that human existence *has* to be informed and guided by ideals which are more than merely achievable personal goals, and that we must operate by moral rules in a game in which we shall always be defeated. There is absolutely no necessity that a life lived in pursuit of good rather than evil will be materially rewarded in this world or a next; such a life does not permit of final achievement and satisfaction. *There is no spiritual nirvana, no final solution, no ultimate certainty; no City of God, no Kingdom of Heaven, no end of history.*

Every inch of moral ground gained will be lost and will have to be re-taken over and over again. Every moving argument will be negated and will have to be restated in a form unanticipated by power; every morally uplifting tale will be culturally silenced or revised and will have to be rewritten in a newly subversive guise.

If this view is seen as unduly bleak, at least it guards against a futile optimism that risks handing the world over to those who know how to exploit it to their advantage. Comforting stories are welcomed by oppressive power as useful ways of maintaining the status quo.

In the past we have been able to take morality only when laced with religion, hitched to a terrifying authority or a fatuous promise of everlasting life. Our task for the twenty-first century is to see that a moral society is one supported by human ideals far more profound, stable and enduring than a childish dependence on supernatural fantasies or the expectation of material reward. The reason why we have to do this is simple and we all know it: no man is an island.

Nothing could suit corporate plutocracy more than for people to believe that the real satisfactions of life stem ultimately from the cultivation of privacy: that subjective well-being, that is to say, is a matter of 'personal growth' *from the inside*. One-dimensional Business culture in fact closes down public space such that the 'real' world (i.e. the world of the market economy) becomes simply a given that people have to accept without question: 'resistance is useless'. If the many can be persuaded that they have no say in the shaping of material reality, and that personal satisfaction is purely a matter of self-doctoring and private consumption, the world is left wide open for exploitation by the few.

When the only public meanings available are the grim and unassailable 'realities' of the market, people are left to scrabble together for themselves makeshift ways of sharing experiences that actually cannot be accommodated within the Business model (an example would be the rituals of grief that have developed rapidly in recent times—impromptu roadside shrines, greater emotional demonstrativeness, etc.). Quite apart from feeling politically impotent (and demonstrating our alienation by shunning the 'democratic' process in unprecedented numbers), we have to cast around for ways of making *communal* sense of experiences that inevitably arise from our existence as embodied beings but are no longer served by abandoned—and often discredited—traditions.

It is of course understandable for people to feel that one answer to the heartlessness of the outside world is to retire into the realm, if not of the inner self, at least of the private life of home and family, etc. However, I suspect that this kind of strategy is built on the false premise that inner space, privacy, is somehow independent of public structure. In fact, if anything, the opposite seems to me to be the case. For individual people, hell is more often to be experienced within the confines of the family (or indeed the agonies of introspection) than it is in the spaces beyond, and public structures of meaning—what one might broadly call cultures—that have evolved over time to accommodate the concerns of embodied human beings may offer an escape from privacy that actually lends meaning and significance to once-private suffering. As I have already indicated, a decent, caring, multi-dimensional public world makes *use* as well as *sense* of private pain and confusion. One of the most tormented and abused, and admirable (a 'hero', see p. 92 above) people I ever met was rescued as child from total perdition by films and books which, among other things, uncovered, to her amazement, the possibility of love.

There can be no doubt that this Business takeover of just about every aspect of life has been successful almost beyond belief, so much so that it is virtually impossible to envisage how the process might be either reversed or overthrown.[20] There was, to be sure, a great deal that was unsatisfactory about the traditional orthodoxies that prevailed before the takeover, and to attempt to return to the intellectual, moral and spiritual institutions we used to know would indeed be retrograde in the worst sense. We need to recover the multidimensionality of public space that we have lost, but without the stuffy authoritarianism and entrenched inequalities that often went with its principal features.

In his brilliant book *The Power Elite*, written almost fifty years ago, C. Wright Mills wrote:

The knowledgeable man in the genuine public is able to turn his personal troubles into social issues, to see their relevance for his community and his community's relevance for them. He understands that what he thinks and feels as personal troubles are very often not only that but problems shared by others and indeed not subject to solution by any one individual but only by modifications of the structure of the groups in which he lives and sometimes the structure of the entire society.

Men in masses are gripped by personal troubles, but they are not aware of their true meaning and source. Men in public confront issues, and they are aware of their terms. It is the task of the liberal institution, as of the liberally educated man, continually to translate troubles into issues and issues into the terms of their human meaning for the individual. In the absence of deep and wide political debate, schools for adults and adolescents could perhaps become hospitable frameworks for just such debate. In a community of publics the task of liberals would be: to keep the public from being overwhelmed; to help produce the disciplined and informed mind that cannot be overwhelmed; to help develop the bold and sensible individual that cannot be sunk by the burdens of mass life. But educational practice has not made knowledge directly relevant to the human need of the troubled person of the twentieth century or to the social practices of the citizen. The citizen cannot now see the roots of his own biases and frustrations, nor think clearly about himself, nor for that matter about anything else. He does not see the frustration of idea, of intellect, by the present organisation of society, and he is not able to meet the tasks now confronting 'the intelligent citizen'.[21]

For people to be able to understand *and act upon* the powers and influences within society that bring about their personal misery and confusion, we need to reopen the ethical space[22] that allows us to share and evaluate our subjective experience in solidarity with others. The structures that will enable this are not *therapeutic*, but *political*.

Figure 5.1 (over) offers a (highly oversimplified) view of how a conventionally left-wing, social democratic political system might theoretically be aimed at creating the kind of personal environment where individuals could flourish as both public and private beings.

It is sobering to reflect that even this relatively modest ideal has become so far out of reach as to as to appear simply absurd. For national governments no longer determine their own policies, and the influences of global corporate plutocracy intrude at every level of social organisation to further their own interests.

In the absence of any traditionally organised opposition, all we can do, perhaps, is resist as best we can. A lot of people are of course already doing this. Informed and committed minorities are often active at local levels to expose

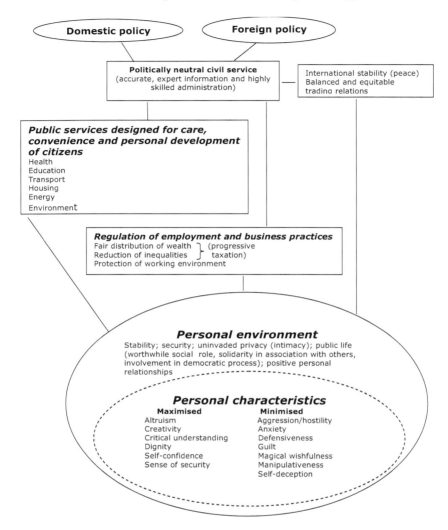

Figure 5.1 Political Space

and combat abuses stemming from, for example, bureaucracies responsible for health, housing, policing, etc. Human rights issues, the exploitation of consumers, and so on, may also arouse the opposition of people otherwise disillusioned with conventional politics and form them into effective campaigning groups.

Even so, it may be wise not to get too excited about the implications of such movements for the wider political scene. Few corporate leaders are likely to lose much sleep over campaigns aimed at encouraging individuals to exercise their will in, for example, areas of consumption that do not directly affect their comfort. Punitive taxes may well bring people out on the streets, but concerns about the ethics of, say, sportswear production in faraway places are likely to have only a slight effect on people's buying habits, if any. However passionately they feel, it is vain to expect that the piecemeal dissent of scattered individuals is going to make much of an impact, and even effective, 'single-issue' action will, not least in view of the tacit interests of popular media, easily be contained within the relatively narrow arena in which it arises. The apparatus of power is too well developed to allow such dissent to get out of hand.

At more distal levels, the Internet has made possible both the dissemination of information and possibilities of communication that have fostered large-scale protests such as those seen in recent years at Seattle and Genoa. These latter—not unlike the student unrest of 1968—have certainly demonstrated that it is possible to move supposedly democratic powers to repressive action, but it is also true that organised power has recourse to such a wide range of resources that it is hard to envisage being able to do much more than provoke it to reveal its coercive base.

This is of course not to say that powerful regimes never collapse: the disintegration of Eastern European communism is still a vivid memory for many of us. But though people caught up in such events may experience them as, for instance, the triumph of good over evil and dance in the streets at what they see as the dawning of a new era ('Things can only get better'!) it is more likely that they are the upshot of seismic economic movements at the most distal reaches of the ordinary person's comprehension. As with so much else, the activist or protester is likely to feel that *involvement* in events is the same as *origination* of them. The masses may well be the instrument of revolution, but they are far less likely to be its cause, and it may take a while to discern who are its true beneficiaries.

One of the easiest mistakes to make is to suppose that persuasion is an important factor in bringing about organised opposition. One of the most potent mythologies of ideological power is that reasoned argument leads to changes of heart, that debate is the engine of change.

In her mordantly compelling *Lugano Report*[23] Susan George vividly draws attention to the inadequacy of rational argument as a means of influencing people. In starting to consider alternatives to the potentially disastrous practices of global capitalism, she writes:

This section has to start on a personal note because frankly, power relations being what they are, I feel at once moralistic and silly proposing alternatives. More times than I care to count I have attended events ending with a rousing declaration about what 'should' or 'must' occur. So many well-meaning efforts so totally neglect the crucial dimension of power that I try to avoid them now unless I think I can introduce an element of realism that might otherwise be absent.

... because I am constantly being asked 'what to do', I begin with some negative suggestions. The first is not to be trapped by the 'should', the 'must' and the 'forehead-slapping school'. Assuming that any change, because it would contribute to justice, equity and peace, need only to be explained to be adopted is the saddest and most irritating kind of naivety.

Many good, otherwise intelligent people seem to believe that once powerful individuals and institutions have actually *understood* the gravity of the crisis (any crisis) and the urgent need for its remedy, they will smack their brows, admit they have been wrong all along and, in a flash of revelation, instantly redirect their behaviour by 180 degrees. While ignorance and stupidity must be given their due, most things come out the way they do because the powerful want them to come out that way.

In other words, most things come out the way they do in accordance with the interests of the powerful. Nowhere is the myth of rationality more obvious than in interviews conducted in television newscasts. Disputants A and B, representing, for example, opposing views on nuclear energy, genetically modified food, immigration policy, etc., attempt to make a rational case for their standpoint and yet are never themselves moved by reason. This is, of course, because they are *interested parties*, and indeed are chosen as such by the interviewers. Their views are formed and maintained by their interests, and any debate is utterly futile because their views will change only when their interests change. The politician 'making a case' for a given course of action is perhaps the purest example of how interest shapes conduct. And because we repress interest in favour of, among other things, a mythology of rationality, politicians, as they struggle to hide interest behind reason, are always revealed as liars.

It is essential to note, however, that politicians are not qualitatively different from the rest of us. In our case also our actions are more easily understandable and predictable from an analysis of our interests in relation to the networks of power we inhabit than they are from our beliefs or 'cognitions'.

This is not to say that reason does not have a place in human society—it is particularly important, as I have tried to show, in the conduct of scientific investigation. But this is a very unusual, artificially created environment needing all kinds of special protection for its survival. If we are to account for the ways in which we act towards each other in the real world, we need to develop a far more sophisticated—and indeed tolerant—understanding of the workings of power and interest.

For many readers, this will, I think, be a very bitter pill to swallow. For among those readers there will be many, I suspect, who strive to live ethically and are responsive to information that enables them the better to do so. For such people it is hard not to conclude that change based on a reasonable appraisal of the good is possible, because it seems to them that that is the way their lives have been lived. But whatever makes it possible for some to criticise their lot, and even to move against the influences that shape it, there will be many more who will be fairly easily ruled by deference to Authority and seduced by make-believe and the deregulation of pleasure.

I anticipate that this last observation will be condemned as 'cynical', but I do think that that would be a mistake. The central argument of this book is, after all, that it is not the personal apprehension of right or reason that moves us to action, but the flow of power and interest within the social networks in which we are caught up. As long as we can be convinced that changing the world is down to individual action, that the political is personal, nothing much will change.

Some people will, I know, find what I'm saying dispiriting, but I in no way feel it incumbent on me (nor do I expect anyone else) to offer solutions—indeed to do so would seem to me simply foolish. The world is in a bloody mess and even though I know, as do many others, what it would look like if it weren't, I have no more viable idea than anyone else how to get there. I do believe, however, that an extremely important step on the way is *to take really seriously the fact that we are a society, not a collection of individuals, and that we live in a real world that is as impervious to optimism as it is to wishfulness.*

It does seem likely, though, that—perhaps in the not too far distant future—the effect on the real world of current economic structures and policies will alter very radically indeed the physical conditions of our existence. Solidary action may once again arise, as it has in the past, from our having nothing to lose but our misery.

Notes

1. Smail, D. 1997. Psychotherapy and tragedy. In House, R. and Totton, N. *Implausible Professions: Arguments for pluralism and autonomy in psychotherapy and counselling*, pp. 159–70. PCCS Books.

2. To take four recent examples, see:
   - Paul Gordon, 2004. Night thoughts of a sceptical therapist. In Paul Gordon and Rosalind Mayo (eds). *Between Psychotherapy and Philosophy*. Whurr Publishers.
   - Peter Lomas, 1999. *Doing Good? Psychotherapy out of its depth*. Oxford University Press.
   - Terry Lynch, 2004. *Beyond Prozac*. PCCS Books.
   - Taiwo Afuape. 2004. Challenge to obscuring difference: being a Black woman psychologist using SELF in therapy. *Journal of Critical Psychology, Counselling and Psychotherapy*, 4, 164–75.

3. The most recent edition of this book forms half of the double volume *The Nature of Unhappiness.* Robinson, 2001.

4. See for example:
   • Roy Bhaskar, 1989. *Reclaiming Reality.* Verso;
   • Ian Burkitt,1991. *Social Selves.* Sage;
   • Margaret S. Archer, 2000. *Being Human.* Cambridge University Press;
   • David J. Nightingale and John Cromby (eds), 1999. *Social Constructionist Psychology* . Open University Press.

5. This may seem obvious now, but it certainly did not to some of the worthiest Victorian social reformers—see for example Elizabeth Gaskell's *North and South*, in which her socialism remains obstinately attached to her protestantism. The present-day therapist, politician, 'communitarian', etc. who links betterment in some form to responsibility in some form is thus still stuck in a century-old mould.

6. A good account can be found in Orford, J. *Community Psychology: Theory and Practice*, Wiley, 1992.

7. Ivan Illich, 1977. *Disabling Professions.* Marion Boyars.

8. Isaac Prilleltensky and Geoffrey Nelson, 2002. *Doing Psychology Critically.* Palgrave.

9. See my review of Prilleltensky and Nelson's book in the *Journal of Community and Applied Social Psychology*, 2003, *13*, 328.

10. Russell Jacoby, 1975. *Social Amnesia: A critique of conformist psychology from Adler to Laing.* Harvester. pp. 139–40.

11. Jürgen Habermas, *The Theory of Communicative Action*, 2 vols., trans. Thomas McCarthy (Boston: Beacon Press, 1984 and 1987) (German edition, 1981).

12 For similar reflections on the state of knowledge and truth in the contemporary world, see Frank Furedi's *Where Have All The Intellectuals Gone?* 2004, Continuum.

13. All this documented in *The Guardian*, 7.2.02

14. This phenomenon is encountered in almost pure form in the volume edited (in utterly good faith but with dismaying results) by Colin Feltham: *Controversies in Psychotherapy and Counselling*, Sage Publications, 1999. For a powerful critique of the corruption of the psychology industry see Tana Dineen's *Manufacturing Victims*, Constable, 1999, and also Susan Hansen, Alec McHoul and Mark Rapley *Beyond Help*, 2003, PCCS Books.

15. Greg Philo and David Miller, 2001. *Market Killing.* Longman.

16. Much of this and the following section has been published in D. Smail, 2004, *Psychotherapy and The Making of Subjectivity.* In Gordon, P. and Mayo, R. (eds), 2004. *Between Psychotherapy and Philosophy*, pp 130–40. London and Philadelphia: Whurr.

17. Richard Rorty, 1980. *Philosophy and the Mirror of Nature.* Blackwell.

18. From the *Statement* of the Centre for Research in Globalisation, as set out in their website at www.globalresearch.ca/

19. Anyone who thinks slavery no longer exists should consult *Disposable People*, by Kevin Bales (Univ. California Press, 1999). Not only is the practice of slavery widespread, but exists on an unprecedented scale. Bales is careful to consider only 'true' slavery—people being forced to work for nothing. People having to work at meaningless jobs for next to nothing is little better.

20. In his book *Decline of the Public*, Polity Press 2004, David Marquand provides an informative account of the rise of public-spiritedness and the public realm in Victorian times, and its fall in our own. He also gives indications of some of the things we need to do to reverse this decline—but perhaps without taking full account of the formidable powers ranged against any such effort.

21. Mills, C.W. 1956. *The Power Elite*. London and New York: Oxford University Press, p. 318.

22. For a masterly, and too neglected, exposition of the concept of ethical space, see the late Roger Poole's *Towards Deep Subjectivity*, 1972, Allen Lane The Penguin Press.

23. Susan George, 1999. *The Lugano Report*. Pluto Press. p. 181.

Epilogue

I know from what is now quite long experience that however explicit a writer tries to make his (in my case) position, he will be understood in a wide variety of ways, some of them very far indeed from his intention.

I try as hard as I can to say what I mean, but I may still find my books placed by booksellers under 'The Occult', or be asked by readers for guidance on *therapeutic* solutions to the world's ills. People often find in books what they want to find—and that may be as much a stimulus to outrage as a panacea.

I know also that serious readers will be left with questions, puzzles, frustrations that I'd like at this stage to attempt to address. And so I would like to end this book by making a more directly personal statement of what I am trying to achieve by writing it.

Since its content has arisen largely out of talking to clinical psychologists and therapists, and indeed is written mainly with them in mind, the first thing I want to emphasise, even if not for the first time, is that I am not trying to destroy therapy, but to put it in its rightful place (which is, in every sense—including the very best—a modest one). However it may sometimes seem, I am not trying to disable people with gloom, but to help make possible a sober confrontation of our difficulties, to pull clinical and therapeutic psychology up from its headlong rush into bogus therapeutic solutions and to open the way to a serious consideration of what I unapologetically consider the scientific issues.

As I have tried to make clear, I do not see the position that I develop here as my invention, but as arising within a tradition to which I see myself as belonging. All I try to do is bring my experience as a clinical psychologist to confirm and elaborate some aspects of that position. I do think, though, that the radicality of the message that I and others seek to convey is easily overlooked. To suggest that *the social* is constitutive of our being, that we are as much creatures of culture as of biology, and that the world in which we live is real, is actually to point to a very fundamental revision of the way we commonly think about ourselves, not only within psychology, but much more generally within wider Western culture. To de-centre the self, to suggest that it is an idealist invention that has no *autonomous* power not only demands that we revise vast areas of received philosophical and psychological opinion, but undermines the very basis of consumer capitalism.

And yet this basic proposition is one that liberal (in the best sense) thinkers are very loath to take, for it seems that by stripping the self, or ego, of its individual autonomy one is indeed robbing us of our freedom and dignity. In the Western tradition at least, left-wing thinkers have tended to stress the individual's free agency rather than attack it.

This, I think, arises from the experience of having been subjugated for most of the twentieth century by positivism and behaviourism, whereby individuals find themselves cast as puppets in a world run by puppet-masters. Behaviourism's principal failing, apart from its narrow oversimplification, was that it wasn't reflexive, i.e. that the scientist was not included among the puppets.

In any case, as I tried to show in Chapter One, many of us reacted to this oppressive ideology by turning to, essentially, more Romantic views of human nature, in which as little restraint as possible was placed on individual freedom.

To suggest that, as embodied social beings, *none* of us has individual autonomy is if anything more radical than behaviourism, but it is also less oppressive, for it places us all in the same boat. More than that, it places us in the same boat as the rest of creation; at some stage we are going to have to abandon our pretensions to mini-god status and recognise that we are subject to the same constraints as other material beings.

What I have tried to do here (particularly in Chapter Two, which I regard as the core of this book) is to suggest one or two tentative steps we might take in psychology to arrive at a more adequate conceptual (I am tempted to say 'technical', but that is probably too strong a term and too easily abused) language in which we can begin to think about the causes of our conduct, as well as of course our subjective distress.

'Romantic' psychology seems more able to swallow drastic pills if they are coated in the sugar of non-Western approaches. De-centring the autonomous subject and calling into question the extent of its agency is in fact doing much the same as, say, Buddhist thought but, I suspect, somehow seems more brutal. But while there are indeed sweeping changes to be made in our basic ideas about ourselves, they do not, I think, violate our fundamental well-being or demand some painful adjustment of our subjective experience. Indeed, I would expect just the opposite to be the case.

To suggest that the subject is more an effect than a cause is not to devalue it, but to direct our attention to the contexts which shape and impinge upon it. For we are not denying the *existence* of subjectivity, only its autonomy. Indeed, we take subjective experience as the very heart of our enterprise, as what 'clinical' psychology is and should be all about. What we do *not* do is make the subject responsible for its own condition.

The individualist ideology that consumer capitalism promotes, and that has enjoyed such a startling resurgence in the past two decades or so, breeds greedy competition, indifference to the plight of others, exploitation, hatred and contempt for the weak. It feeds personal arrogance and encourages us to confuse the acquisition of wealth and power with virtue. Perhaps even more important than coercion, it maintains its power through a range of seductive myths that cynically engage our interests. Despite the falsity of the make-believe world it creates, it is highly effective—and immensely damaging, to societies as to individuals.

Even if much of what I have written seems despairing (and I'm glad to say not *everyone* sees it that way!) I think that the consequences of abandoning a literally self-centred psychology would increase freedom and dignity rather than diminish them.

To recognise that being who we are is not a matter of personal choice, to acknowledge that well-being is more a matter of providence than of will, that whether we are happy or sad, good or bad, depends greatly on contexts over which we have, for the most part, no direct control, would be to direct us to forms of relating to each other that have all but dropped out of sight. To take ourselves seriously as *social* beings, embodied in a real world that resists mere wishfulness, would encourage modesty, appreciation of good fortune, compassion, recognition of commonality. Not only that, but it would I think reflect more accurately our actual experience: if we accepted ourselves as creatures who *mediate* rather than *originate* environmental influence, we'd spend far less time than we do feeling slightly puzzled and surprised at the unpredictability of our feelings and actions and the unreliability of our intentions.

The flip-side of capitalist ideology's sentimental make-believe and the magical voluntarism that supports it is to be seen all too easily in the brutal exploitation, oppression and subjugation of the weak by the strong, within as well as between societies. It is not only Middle Eastern cities that are laid waste in the new barbarism, but millions upon millions of individual lives across the globe.

Repudiation of magic is not the same thing as disenchantment. Nothing, indeed, could be more apocalyptically stripped of human pity and hope than the real world that festers behind the screens of make-believe spun so adeptly by the neo-liberal dream-weavers. In order to rehabilitate the world, human beings will need to structure their ideals in accordance with the realities of their mutual interdependence. To this end magic is useless, but utopianism— forms of re-enchantment that depend on human rather than divine effort—is not. In the long run we stand a better chance of being able to make a habitable world conform to our ideals than we do of realising our greedy fantasies of personal power.

Imperfect species that we are, we may never achieve what in principle perhaps we could; but when it comes to peace, harmony, understanding and mutual support (just some of the bases of personal well-being) we could certainly do better than we are at present. Psychologists and psychotherapists might have an honourable, though modest part to play in such a project—if only by helping to expose the factors that militate against it.

Index

PCCS Books — publishers of counselling, psychotherapy and critical psychology texts

CRITICAL PSYCHOLOGY DIVISION

Commissioning Editors: Craig Newnes and Guy Holmes

This is Madness
A critical look at psychiatry and the future of mental health services
Edited by **Craig Newnes**, **Guy Holmes** and **Cailzie Dunn**
ISBN 978 1 898 05925 7, 1999

This is Madness Too
Critical perspectives on mental health services
Edited by **Craig Newnes**, **Guy Holmes** and **Cailzie Dunn**
ISBN 978 1 898 05937 0, 2001

Personality as Art
Artistic approaches in psychology
Peter Chadwick
ISBN 978 1 898 05935 6, 2001

Spirituality and Psychotherapy
Edited by **Simon King-Spooner** and **Craig Newnes**
ISBN 978 1 898 05939 4, 2001

Beyond Help
A consumers' guide to psychology
Susan Hansen, Alec McHoul and **Mark Rapley**
ISBN 978 1 898 05954 7, 2003

The Gene Illusion
Genetic research in psychiatry and psychology under the microscope
Jay Joseph
ISBN 978 1 898 05947 9, 2003

Violence and Society
Making sense of madness and badness
Elie Godsi
ISBN 978 1 898 05962 2, 2004

Beyond Prozac
Healing mental suffering
Dr Terry Lynch
ISBN 978 1 898 05963 9, 2004

Making and Breaking Children's Lives
Edited by **Craig Newnes** and **Nick Radcliffe**
ISBN 978 1 898 05970 7, 2005

www.pccs-books.co.uk

PCCS Books

Independent publishing for
independent thinkers

www.pccs-books.co.uk